GOD'S WOR

GOD'S WORD
Men's Words

J. DAVID PRICE

THANKFUL BOOKS

First published 2006

Published by Thankful Books
70 Milton Road, Eastbourne, East Sussex
BN21 1SS, UK

ISBN-13: 978 1 905084 08 1
ISBN-10: 1 905084 08 0

Book design and production for the publisher by Bookprint Creative Services <www.bookprint.co.uk>.
Printed in Great Britain.

Preface

This book of daily readings contains a personal collection of quotes (men's words), which have been gathered together from various sources over a period of thirty years. At the time they were (and still are) particularly meaningful. Where known I have quoted the author, but this has not always been possible and I apologise to anyone whose words are included but I have failed to acknowledge. I am particularly indebted to the writings of Selwyn Hughes of Crusade for World Revival and I am grateful to the Oswald Chambers Publications Association Limited for permission to use quotations from Oswald Chambers.

The quotes have been grouped together under various headings which are arranged alphabetically. They are accompanied by relevant biblical verses (God's Word). Space has been provided for individual notes and some pages for a personal prayer diary are included at the back.

The book is intended to be used systematically on a daily basis, perhaps in those spare moments caught in a traffic jam or just waiting for a kettle to boil. It can also be dipped into on a subject basis. In compiling this volume of daily devotions, I trust that the combined wisdom of the created and the Creator will challenge, encourage and inspire the reader.

Preface

Adversity/Affliction

Our times of adversity are often the times we become more conscious of the Lord's presence and power.

It sometimes takes an upset to set us up.

Don't forget in the darkness what you have learnt in the light.

---

1 Peter 5:7 Leave all your worries with him, because he cares for you. GNB.

Lam. 3:22 The steadfast love of the LORD never ceases; his mercies never come to an end;

2 Tim. 1:8 Therefore do not be ashamed of the testimony about our Lord, nor of me (Paul) his prisoner, but share in suffering for the gospel by the power of God . . .

Notes:

January 2nd

Adversity/Affliction

We need to have the mindset that says; as it is most likely I cannot avoid adversity, I will, with God's help, seek to use it.

A dark tunnel is often the best way of getting around a hill.

Pain can be God's megaphone to us *C. S. Lewis*

---

2 Cor. 8:2 . . . for in a severe test of affliction, their (the churches of Macedonia) abundance of joy and their extreme poverty have overflowed in a wealth of generosity on their part.

2 Chron. 20:9 If disaster comes upon us, the sword, judgement, or pestilence, or famine, we will stand before this house and before you – for your name is in this house – and cry out to you in our affliction, and you will hear and save.

Notes:

Adversity/Affliction

Life's trials should make us better – not bitter.

Out of every mess, God is able to make a message.

I know that no disease, no accident, could take anything away from me that I need in order to fulfil the purposes the Creator had for my life. *Robert C. Barnes*

---

1 Thess. 3:7 for this reason, brothers, in all our distress and affliction we have been comforted about you through your faith.

Isaiah 53:4 Surely he has borne our griefs and carried our sorrows; yet we esteemed him stricken, smitten by God, and afflicted.

Psalm 73:26 My mind and my body may grow weak, but God is my strength; he is all I ever need. GNB.

Notes:

January 4th

Adversity/Affliction

I glance at my difficulties, but I gaze at God.

Paul had a thorn in his flesh, but nobody knows what it was. If we had a thorn in the flesh, everybody would know what it was.

Jesus never offered us a smooth journey, just a safe arrival.

Ecclesiastes 7:14 In the day of prosperity be joyful, and in the day of adversity consider: God has made the one as well as the other . . .

Psalm 25:18 Consider my affliction and my trouble, and forgive all my sins.

Hebrews 4:15,16 For we do not have a high priest who is unable to sympathize with our weaknesses, but one who in every respect has been tempted as we are, yet without sin.

Notes:

Adversity/Affliction

When testings come we are purified, but when prosperity comes we are vulnerable.

You should never let adversity get you down, except on your knees.

The problems ahead of us are never as great as the power behind us.

Isaiah 53:3 He was despised and rejected by men; a man of sorrows, and acquainted with grief; and as one from whom men hide their faces he was despised, and we esteemed him not.

Hebrews 11:25 . . . (Moses) choosing rather to be mistreated with the people of God than to enjoy the fleeting pleasures of sin.

Notes:

January 6th

Adversity/Affliction

God can turn setbacks into springboards, obstacles into opportunities.

Whenever we get into spiritual difficulties we have three resources – the Word of God, the Spirit of God and the people of God. *Selwyn Hughes*

Trouble is often a blessing in disguise.

Nahum 1:7 The LORD is good; he protects his people in times of trouble; he takes care of those who turn to him. GNB.

Psalm 46:1 God is our refuge and strength, a very present help in trouble.

Matthew 11:28 Come to me (Jesus), all who labour and are heavy laden, and I will give you rest.

Notes:

Adversity/Affliction

The God of the stars is also the God of the scars.

We sometimes have to be put on our backs before we can look up into His face.

God's wilderness is always to be preferred to man's garden.

Psalm 31:7 I will rejoice and be glad in your steadfast love, because you have seen my affliction; you have known the distress of my soul . . .

Matthew 26:39 And going a little farther he (Jesus) fell on his face and prayed, saying, "My Father, if it be possible, let this cup pass from me; nevertheless, not as I will, but as you will."

2 Cor. 4:17 For this slight momentary affliction is preparing for us an eternal weight of glory beyond all comparison . . .

Notes:

January 8th

Adversity/Affliction

God will not always deliver us from tragedy, but deliverance in God is not a killjoy but a filljoy.

When life hits a Christian on the chin, it tilts his face upwards to look on the face of God.

Psalm 40:2 He (the LORD) drew me up from the pit of destruction, out of the miry bog, and set my feet upon a rock, making my steps secure.

John 14:1 Let not your hearts be troubled. Believe in God; believe also in me (Jesus).

Notes:

Adversity/Affliction

Experience is the greatest of all teachers, though his fees are sometimes heavy.

In God's service, everything can be used; in every obstacle there is an opportunity, in every difficulty a door and in every stumbling block a stepping stone. *Selwyn Hughes*

---

2 Cor. 4:8,9 We are afflicted in every way, but not crushed; perplexed, but not driven to despair; persecuted, but not forsaken; struck down, but not destroyed;

Psalm 34:18 The LORD is near to the broken-hearted and saves the crushed in spirit.

Notes:

January 10th

Adversity/Affliction

Adversity is one of the greatest teachers, and God uses it to polish His jewels.

When you are tired you are attacked by ideas you thought you had conquered long ago.

God has a wonderful way of disguising opportunities as problems.

James 1:12 Blessed is the man who remains steadfast under trial, for when he has stood the test he will receive the crown of life, which God has promised to those who love him.

Psalm 42:5 Why am I so sad? Why am I so troubled? I will put my hope in God, and once again I will praise him, my saviour and my God. GNB.

Notes:

Anger

Anger is righteous when it flows as a passionate concern at what is happening to others and not as a grudge at what is happening to us.

When Christians quarrel, the devil remains neutral and provides ammunition to both sides.

Anger is usually the result of a goal we are pursuing becoming blocked.

James 1:19 Know this, my beloved brothers: let every person be quick to hear, slow to speak, slow to anger;

Psalm 103:8 The LORD is merciful and gracious, slow to anger and abounding in steadfast love.

Matthew 5:22 But I (Jesus) say to you that everyone who is angry with his brother will be liable to judgement;

Psalm 37:8 Don't give in to worry or anger; it only leads to trouble. GNB.

Notes:

January 12th

Anger

Anger is a choice.

When God gets angry, He doesn't stop loving.

If anger is not dealt with, Satan will quickly move in.

Dealing with anger:

1. First acknowledge anger.
2. Choose not to let it get out of control.
3. Carefully and prayerfully think through the best way of dealing with the situation which aroused the anger in the first place.

Eph. 4:26 Be angry and do not sin; do not let the sun go down on your anger . . .

Ecclesiastes 7:9 Be not quick in your spirit to become angry, for anger lodges in the bosom of fools.

Eph. 4:31 Let all bitterness and wrath and anger and clamour and slander be put away from you, along with all malice.

Notes:

Bless

The word bless means a state of happiness, of well being; to speak well of, to give thanks.

God's blessings are there to be taken, but they are never to be taken for granted.

Never confuse numbers or busy-ness with blessing.

Eph. 1:3 Blessed be the God and Father of our Lord Jesus Christ, who has blessed us in Christ with every spiritual blessing in the heavenly places . . .

Luke 11:28 But he (Jesus) said, "Blessed rather are those who hear the word of God and keep it!"

James 1:12 Blessed is the man who remains steadfast under trial, for when he has stood the test he will receive the crown of life, which God has promised to those who love him.

Notes:

January 14th

Bless

Blessing always follows obedience and there is no blessing without obedience.

God gives His blessing when He finds an empty vessel.

When we look within we are depressed. When we look around, we are impressed. When we look at Jesus, we are blessed.

Romans 12:14 Bless those who persecute you; bless and do not curse them.

Psalm 128:4 Behold, thus shall the man be blessed who fears the LORD.

Matthew 5:8 Blessed are the pure in heart, for they shall see God.

James 1:25 But those who look closely into the perfect law that sets people free, who keep on paying attention to it and do not simply listen and then forget it, but put it into practice – they will be blessed by God in what they do. GNB.

Notes:

Bless

How often we purr when we receive God's blessing, but growl when chastised for sin.

What a mercy it is that God blesses us for what we are today, and does not hold the failure of tomorrow against us.

John 20:29 Jesus said to him (Thomas), "Have you believed because you have seen me? Blessed are those who have not seen and yet have believed."

Acts 20:35 . . . remember the words of the Lord Jesus, how he himself said, "It is more blessed to give than to receive."

Notes:

January 16th

Christian/Christianity

A Christian is a person who acknowledges and lives under the word of God. *J. I. Packer*

If Christ is the centre of our lives, the circumference will take care of itself.

The greatest test of a Christian is: what is the person like at home?

Gal. 2:20 I (Paul) have been crucified with Christ. It is no longer I who live, but Christ who lives in me. And the life I now live in the flesh I live by faith in the Son of God, who loved me and gave himself for me.

1 Peter 4:16 Yet if anyone suffers as a Christian, let him not be ashamed, but let him glorify God in that name.

Notes:

Christian/Christianity

There is no part of our lives that is exempt from His claims, and there is no time or place in which we can temporarily relinquish our Christian faith. *David Porter*

A Christian is one who by word and deed says; "Let me commend my Saviour to you".

A Christian is someone who has eternal life.

Romans 8:16 The Spirit himself bears witness with our spirit that we are children of God . . .

John 10:27 My sheep hear my voice, and I know them, and they follow me.

Eph. 4:11,12 And he (Jesus) gave the apostles, the prophets, the evangelists, the pastors and teachers, to equip the saints for the work of ministry, for building up the body of Christ . . .

Notes:

January 18th

Christian/Christianity

A Christian is someone who knows that his or her salvation was planned in eternity, has entered into it through faith in Christ, is utterly different from the world, and enjoys a continuing relationship with the Lord Jesus Christ.

The acid test of Christianity is obedience.

Eph. 1:4,5 Because of his love God had already decided that through Jesus Christ he would make us his sons and daughters – this was his pleasure and purpose. GNB.

Phil. 2:14,15 Do all things without grumbling or questioning, that you may be blameless and innocent, children of God without blemish in the midst of a crooked and twisted generation, among whom you shine as lights in the world . . .

Notes:

Christian/Christianity

To be a Christian means to forgive the inexcusable, because God has forgiven the inexcusable in us.

C. S. Lewis

A lot of Christians have just enough religion to make them miserable in a dance hall, but not enough to keep them happy in a prayer meeting. *D. L. Moody*

A Christian is a person in whom Christ lives.

Luke 9:23 And he (Jesus) said to all, "If anyone would come after me, let him deny himself and take up his cross daily and follow me."

Isaiah 43:1 But now thus says the LORD, he who created you, O Jacob, he who formed you, O Israel: "Fear not, for I have redeemed you; I have called you by name, you are mine."

Notes:

Christian/Christianity

A Christian is one who comes to Christ. Before he came, however, he was a gift from the Father to the Son.

There is no life without death, no gain without pain, no crown without a cross and no victory except through surrender. *Selwyn Hughes*

---

1 Peter 2:21 For to this you have been called, because Christ also suffered for you, leaving you an example, so that you might follow in his steps.

Gal. 4:6 And because you are sons, God has sent the Spirit of his Son into our hearts, crying, "Abba! Father!"

John 1:12 But to all who did receive him (Jesus), who believed in his name, he gave the right to become children of God . . .

Notes:

Christian/Christianity

When a Christian can say he has Christ in his heart, and offers a practical obedience as evidence and ground of this, he too wins many for the Lord. *Archbishop Temple*

Other religions are sets of swimming instructions for a drowning man. Christianity is a life preserver.

Deut. 14:2 For you are a people holy to the Lord your God, and the LORD has chosen you to be a people for his treasured possession, out of all the peoples who are on the face of the earth.

Hebrews 10:25 Let us not give up the habit of meeting together, as some are doing. Instead, let us encourage one another all the more, since you see that the Day of the Lord is coming nearer. GNB.

Notes:

January 22nd

Christian/Christianity

Christianity has its creeds, but is not a creed. It has its doctrines, but is not a doctrine. It has its rites and ceremonies, but it is not a rite or ceremony. It has its institutions but is not an institution. At its centre is a person. Christianity is Christ.

Acts 26:18 You are to open their eyes and turn them from the darkness to the light and from the power of Satan to God, so that through their faith in me they will have their sins forgiven and receive their place among God's chosen people. GNB.

Romans 8:29 For those whom he foreknew he also predestined to be conformed to the image of his Son, in order that he might be the firstborn among many brothers.

Notes:

Christian/Christianity

The victorious Christian life is a series of new beginnings.
Alexander Whyte

Christianity is that religion that puts a face and flesh on God.

No cross – no Christianity.

A Christian is a person who, when he gets to the end of his rope, ties a knot and hangs on. *Oral Roberts*

Eph. 5:8 . . . for at one time you were darkness, but now you are light in the Lord. Walk as children of light . . .

1 Cor. 6:15 Do you not know that your bodies are members of Christ?

Gal. 3:26 . . . for in Christ Jesus you are all sons of God, through faith.

Notes:

January 24th

Christian/Christianity

Religion is man's search for God. Christianity is God's search for man.

A Christian is one who cares. *Baron von Huegal*

The heart of Christianity is the matter of the heart.

Christianity is the science of getting on well with others according to Jesus Christ.

---

1 Thess. 1:9 For they themselves report concerning us the kind of reception we had among you, and how you turned to God form idols to serve the living and true God . . .

Eph. 5:29,30 For no one ever hated his own flesh, but nourishes and cherishes it, just as Christ does the church, because we are members of his body.

Romans 8:14 For all who are led by the Spirit of God are sons of God.

Notes:

Christian/Christianity

A Christian is like a tea bag – he is not worth much until he has been through some hot water.

A Christian life is not our responsibility, but our response to His ability.
Selwyn Hughes

Christians are not made, they are in the making.

Phil. 2:1,2 Your life in Christ makes you strong, and his love comforts you. You have fellowship with the Spirit, and you have kindness and compassion for one another. I urge you, then, to make me completely happy by having the same thoughts, sharing the same love, and being one in soul and mind. GNB.

Notes:

January 26th

Christian/Christianity

Christianity is humane action for Jesus's sake at cost to myself.

A Christian is one who is a partaker of Christ's nature, of Christ's life, His triumph and glory.

A Christian is a person in whom Christ lives.

Col. 2:19 . . . Under Christ's control the whole body (the Church) is nourished and held together by its joints and ligaments, and it grows as God wants it to grow. GNB.

Acts 2:42 And they (the believers) devoted themselves to the apostles teaching and fellowship, to the breaking of bread and the prayers.

Notes:

The Church

The Church is a society of unlimited caring.

A body of new-born people who know and love Christ as Saviour, submit to Him as head, relate to their leadership and to each other as fellow members, and each play their God-given part in the Church's life and witness.

---

1 Peter 2:5 . . . you yourselves like living stones are being built up as a spiritual house, to be a holy priesthood, to offer spiritual sacrifices acceptable to God through Jesus Christ.

Romans 12:5 . . . so we, though many, are one body in Christ, and individually members one of another.

Romans 8:16 The Spirit himself bears witness with our spirit that we are children of God . . .

Notes:

January 28th

The Church

The Church is a company of believers, born of the Spirit, justified by faith and evidencing the fruit of the Spirit in their lives.

When the world is at its worst, Christians are at their best.

No corporate life – no Christian life. *D. L. Moody*

Eph. 2:19,20,21 So then you are no longer strangers and aliens, but you are fellow citizens with the saints and members of the household of God, built on the foundation of the apostles and prophets, Christ Jesus himself being the cornerstone, in whom the whole structure, being joined together, grows into a holy temple in the Lord.

1 Cor. 12:27 Now you are the body of Christ and individually members of it.

Notes:

The Church

The Church is a community of people brought into being and maintained by the influence of the Holy Spirit and the Word. The Church is not a society for the perfect, but a hospital for those who are being made whole under Jesus the physician.

Often simply a group of individuals touching elbows on Sunday.

Selwyn Hughes

Col. 1:18 And he (Jesus) is the head of the body, the church. He is the beginning, the firstborn from the dead, that in everything he might be pre-eminent.

1 John 5:2 By this we know that we love the children of God, when we love God and obey his commandments.

Eph. 1:22,23 God put all things under Christ's feet and gave him to the church as supreme Lord over all things. The church is Christ's body, the completion of him who himself completes all things everywhere. GNB.

Notes:

January 30th

The Church

The Church of God cannot be destroyed by its enemies from without, but what about the enemies within?

Churches do not grow by addition, they grow by nutrition.

God has put the Church in the world, but the devil has put the world into the Church.

Psalm 133:1 Behold, how good and pleasant it is when brothers dwell in unity!

Eph. 4:11,12 It was he (Jesus) who "gave gifts"; he appointed some to be apostles, others to be prophets, others to be evangelists, others to be pastors and teachers. He did this to prepare all God's people for the work of Christian service, in order to build up the body of Christ. GNB.

Notes:

Confession

There is a confession of faith and a confession of sin.

Confession means to say the same thing about a sin that God does.

Confession must be wholehearted, without anything held back.

Proverbs 28:13 Whoever conceals his transgressions will not prosper, but he who confesses and forsakes them will obtain mercy.

2 John 7 For many deceivers have gone out into the world, those who do not confess the coming of Jesus Christ in the flesh.

Notes:

February 1st

Confession

Confession must involve an examination of conscience, sorrow and a determination to avoid sin.

Real confession takes place when we open up our whole being to God, conscious and unconscious; the lower reaches as well as the upper reaches. *Selwyn Hughes*

Romans 10:9 . . . if you confess with your mouth that Jesus is Lord and believe in your heart that God raised him from the dead, you will be saved.

1 John 4:15 Whoever confesses that Jesus is the Son of God, God abides in him, and he in God.

Notes:

Confession

Confessing wrong actions without confessing the underlying attitudes is as helpful as continually sweeping away a cobweb and letting the spider remain.

Selwyn Hughes

Confession must be always as wide as the circle of offence.

James 5:16 Therefore, confess your sins to one another and pray for one another, that you may be healed.

1 John 1:9 If we confess our sins, he is faithful and just to forgive us our sins and to cleanse us from all unrighteousness.

Notes:

February 3rd

Conscience

Conscience is a feeling of right and wrong and a compulsion to do right.

The conscience will not go wrong if it operates against the background of this important question – what would Jesus approve?

Conscience is knowledge shared with oneself.

An African Christian said, "Conscience is a sharp knife in the belly."

Hebrews 9:14 . . . how much more will the blood of Christ, who through the eternal Spirit offered himself without blemish to God, purify our conscience from dead works to serve the living God.

Hebrews 10:22 . . . let us draw near with a true heart in full assurance of faith, with our hearts sprinkled clean from an evil conscience . . .

Notes:

Conversion

Conversion is the change, gradual or sudden, by which we, who are the children of the first birth, through a physical birth into a physical world, become children of the second birth, through a spiritual birth into a spiritual world.

Conversion will involve the slaying of the beast within.

Ezekiel 18:30 Therefore I will judge you, O house of Israel, every one according to his ways, declares the Lord GOD. Repent and turn from all your transgressions, lest iniquity be your ruin.

Eph. 2:4 But God, being rich in mercy, because of the great love with which he loved us, even when we were dead in our trespasses, made us alive together with Christ . . .

Notes:

February 5th

Conversion

Theoretically, when a man commits himself to Christ he commits all, but, practically speaking, most men find they have to give Him one area of their lives at a time.

J. White

When Jesus calls a man, he bids him come and die.

Matthew 18:3 . . . and (Jesus) said, "Truly, I say to you, unless you turn and become like children, you will never enter the kingdom of heaven."

Isaiah 55:7 . . . let the wicked forsake his way, and the unrighteous man his thoughts; let him return to the LORD, that he may have compassion on him, and to our God, for he will abundantly pardon.

Notes:

Conversion

It is not the phenomena that surround conversion (instant or gradual) which make it valid, it is by your fruit. After all, the best evidence you are alive is never your birth certificate.

Selwyn Hughes

Conversion isn't turning over a new leaf, it is turning over a new life.

John 3:5 Jesus answered, "Truly, truly, I say to you, unless one is born of water and the Spirit, he cannot enter the kingdom of God."

Acts 3:19 Repent therefore, and turn again, that your sins may be blotted out . . .

2 Cor. 5:17 Therefore, if anyone is in Christ, he is a new creation. The old has passed away; behold, the new has come.

Notes:

February 7th

Conversion

Conversion is a change in character and life followed by an active change of allegiance.

Conversion is the change, gradual or sudden, by which we pass from the kingdom of self to the kingdom of God.

Conversion gives a new direction, a new spirit, a new sphere of living.

---

1 Peter 1: 22,23 . . . love one another earnestly from a pure heart, since you have been born again. . . .

Eph. 5:8,10 . . . for at one time you were darkness, but now you are light in the Lord. Walk as children of light . . . and try to discern what is pleasing to the Lord.

Notes:

Covenant

Covenant = testament = will. Only valid after death – the executor is the Holy Spirit.

A covenant is based on unlimited responsibility: a contract is based on limited liability.

The partial and temporary has been superseded by the perfect and eternal.

---

1 Cor. 11:25 In the same way also he (Jesus) took the cup, after supper, saying, "This cup is the new covenant in my blood. Do this, as often as you drink it, in remembrance of me."

Notes:

February 9th

The Cross

The cross lifts us out of sin, and lifts sin out of us.

He who has been on the cross for us has promised to be under the cross with us. *B. D. Johns*

The cross is God's magnet to draw men to him.

---

1 Peter 2:24 Christ himself carried our sins in his body to the cross, so that we might die to sin and live for righteousness. GNB.

Phil. 2:8 And being found in human form, he humbled himself by becoming obedient to the point of death, even death on a cross.

Notes:

The Cross

The cross is not something we are unable to avoid, but something we face and pick up.

Taking up our cross involves a daily commitment to serving Christ, which carries with it a sense of disgrace and shame.

Selwyn Hughes

No cross, no crown. *William Penn*

Luke 14:27 Whoever does not bear his own cross and come after me cannot be my disciple.

Gal. 6:14 But far be it from me to boast except in the cross of our Lord Jesus Christ . . .

Notes:

February 11th

Death

Death for a believer is nothing more than the anteroom to glory.

Life is sweet, and death bitter, but eternal life is more sweet and eternal death more bitter. *Bishop Hooper*

Teach me to live that I may dread the grave as little as my bed.

Phil. 1:21 For to me (Paul) to live is Christ, and to die is gain.

Hebrews 2:14 Since therefore the children share in flesh and blood, he himself likewise partook of the same things, that through death he might destroy the one who has power of death, that is, the devil . . .

John 11:25 Jesus said to her (Martha), "I am the resurrection and the life. Whoever believes in me, though he die, yet shall he live . . ."

Notes:

Death

When it comes your time to die, be sure that all you need to do is die.

Jim Elliot

When Christ calls a man, He bids him come and die.

Dietrich Bonhoeffer

I hope death finds me planting my cabbages, not so much caring about death as about the imperfect state of my garden.

Michael de Montaigne
(16th century essayist)

Romans 6:23 For the wages of sin is death, but the free gift of God is eternal life in Christ Jesus our Lord.

Phil. 2:8 And being found in human form, he humbled himself by becoming obedient to the point of death, even death on a cross.

Hebrews 9:27 Everyone must die once, and after that be judged by God. GNB.

Notes:

February 13th

Death

It matters not how a man dies, but how he lives. The act of dying is not of importance, it lasts so short a time.

Samuel Johnson

A daughter asked her Scottish father if he needed the Bible read to him as he lay dying. "Nae lassie" he said, "I thatched my house before the storm began".

Romans 8:6 To set the mind on the flesh is death, but to set the mind on the Spirit is life and peace.

Romans 14:8 If we live, we live to the Lord, and if we die, we die to the Lord. So then, whether we live or whether we die, we are the Lord's.

Psalm 23:4 Even though I walk through the valley of the shadow of death, I will fear no evil, for you are with me; your rod and your staff, they comfort me.

Notes:

Death

There is nothing discreditable in dying, I've known the most respectable people do it. *C. S. Lewis*

Death – not a foe to be faced, but simply moving from one house to another.

When I die I shall change my place, but not my company.
John Preston
(a Puritan)

Romans 8:10 But if Christ lives in you, the Spirit is life for you because you have been put right with God, even though your bodies are going to die because of sin. GNB.

1 Cor. 15:51,52 . . . We shall not all sleep, but we shall all be changed . . . For the trumpet will sound, and the dead will be raised imperishable, and we shall be changed.

Notes:

February 15th

Devil/Satan

Satan has to row his boat down God's waterways: he has none of his own.

Whatever poison Satan produces, God turns it into medicine for the elect. *John Calvin*

If Satan has any power over us, it is only because we let him.

---

1 Peter 5:8 Be alert, be on the watch! Your enemy, the Devil, roams round like a roaring lion, looking for someone to devour. GNB.

Eph. 6:11 Put on the whole armour of God, that you may be able to stand against the schemes of the devil.

2 Cor. 11:14 . . . for even Satan disguises himself as an angel of light.

Notes:

Devil/Satan

Men don't believe in the devil now like their fathers used to do.
They reject one creed because it's old, for another because it's new.
But who dogs the steps of the toiling saints, who spreads the net for his feet.
Who sows the tares in the world's broad fields, where the Saviour sows the wheat?

(Continued tomorrow)

---

2 Cor. 12:7 But to keep me (Paul) from being puffed up with pride because of the many wonderful things I saw, I was given a painful physical ailment, which acts as Satan's messenger to beat me and keep me from being proud. GNB.

James 4:7 Submit yourselves therefore to God. Resist the devil, and he will flee from you.

Notes:

February 17th

Devil/Satan

(Continued from yesterday)

They may say the devil has never lived;
  They may say the devil has gone,
But simple people would like to know –
  Who carries his business on?

When God is at work, Satan is surely alongside.

Hebrews 2:14 Since the children, as he calls them, are people of flesh and blood, Jesus himself became like them and shared their human nature. He did this so that through his death he might destroy the Devil, who has the power over death, and in this way set free those who were slaves all their lives because of their fear of death. GNB.

Notes:

Devil/Satan

Before you became a Christian, Satan knew exactly where you lived, but the moment you committed yourself to Christ, he underlined your address in red ink.

Satan trembles when he sees, the weakest saint upon his knees.
William Cowper

Mark 4:15 Some people are like the seeds that fall along the path; as soon as they hear the message, Satan comes and takes it away. GNB.

Eph. 4:27 . . . give no opportunity to the devil.

Notes:

February 19th

Discipleship

Disciple means a pupil, a learner.

Salvation is free, but discipleship will cost you everything you have. *Billy Graham*

I can never be a true disciple until I see my discipleship in terms, not of what I own, but of what I owe.

Luke 14:27,33 "Those who do not carry their own cross and come after me (Jesus) cannot be my disciples . . . none of you can be my disciple unless you give up everything you have." GNB.

John 8:31 So Jesus said to the Jews who had believed in him, "If you abide in my word, you are truly my disciples . . ."

Notes:

Doubt

Doubt is to take two positions on something or to have a divided heart.

Doubt is a state of mind in suspension between faith and unbelief, so that it is neither of them wholly and it is only each partly.
Os Guinness

Doubt is not the same as unbelief.

Matthew 14:31 Jesus immediately reached out his hand and took hold of him (Peter), saying to him, "O you of little faith, why did you doubt?"

Jude 22 And have mercy on those who doubt;

Notes:

February 21st

Evangelist/Evangelism

The presentation of the whole Christ, for the whole man, by the whole Church, into the whole world.

Evangelism is just one beggar telling another where to find food. *D. J. Niles*

Evan-jelly fish – folk with no spiritual vertebrae.

Evangelism is not complete until the evangelised become evangelists. *Billy Graham*

Mark 6:7 And he called the twelve and began to send them out two by two, and gave them authority over the unclean spirits.

2 Tim. 4:5 As for you, always be sober-minded, endure suffering, do the work of an evangelist, fulfil your ministry.

Matthew 28:19 Go therefore and make disciples of all nations, baptizing them in the name of the Father and of the Son and of the Holy Spirit . . .

Notes:

Evangelist/Evangelism

Evangelism is the communicating of the Gospel in order that people may be converted and so added to the church of Jesus Christ.

Evangelism is sensitively rubbing one's spiritual finger along the edge of a person's soul, feeling for areas of obvious need. *Selwyn Hughes*

An evangelist enlarges the Church both by presenting the Gospel and by inspiring others to reach out to their non-Christian friend.

Isaiah 52:7 How beautiful upon the mountains are the feet of him who brings good news, who publishes peace, who brings good news of happiness, who publishes salvation, who says to Zion, "Your God reigns".

Acts 1:8 But you will receive power when the Holy Spirit has come upon you, and you will be my witnesses in Jerusalem and in all Judea and Samaria, and to the end of the earth.

Notes:

February 23rd

Faith

Faith has to do with God and his eternal infallible word, and connects with the soul of God who gives it. Faith looks upwards and is encouraged. Faith has to do with God's unchanging truth and Christ's eternal enduring sacrifice. Feeling however is occupied with self, looks inward and is discouraged. It has to do with one's own fluctuating condition.

C. H. Spurgeon

---

1 Tim. 3:9 They (deacons) must hold the mystery of the faith with a clear conscience.

Isaiah 7:9 . . . If you are not firm in faith, you will not be firm at all.

1 Tim. 6:12 Run your best in the race of faith, and win eternal life for yourself; for it was to this life that God called you when you firmly professed your faith before many witnesses. GNB.

Notes:

Faith

Faith is the art of holding on to things our reason has once accepted in spite of our changing mood. *C. S. Lewis*

Forsaking All I Trust Him

Faith has three components; knowledge, self-committal and trust.

---

1 Peter 1:6,7 Be glad about this, even though it may now be necessary for you to be sad for a while because of the many kinds of trials you suffer. Their purpose is to prove that your faith is genuine. Even gold, which can be destroyed, is tested by fire; and so your faith, which is much more precious than gold, must also be tested, so that it may endure. GNB.

Notes:

February 25th

Faith

Faith sees the invisible, believes the incredible and receives the impossible.

When faith remembers the agony of the cross, it learns to hate all that put our Saviour there.

Faith is a continuous principle.

Faith is an inner conviction that banks on the *bona fide* promises of God.

Phil. 3:8,9 Indeed, I count everything as loss because of the surpassing worth of knowing Christ Jesus my Lord. For his sake I have suffered the loss of all things and count them as rubbish, in order that I may gain Christ and be found in him, not having a righteousness of my own that comes from the law, but that which comes through faith in Christ, the righteousness from God that depends on faith.

Notes:

Faith

Faith perseveres. It needs work if it is to grow.

The life of faith is not a life of mounting up with wings, but a life of walking and not fainting. *Oswald Chambers*

Never let your faith depend on a particular thing happening. Let your faith be in God.

Matthew 6:30 But if God so clothes the grass of the field, which today is alive and tomorrow is thrown into the oven, will he not much more clothe you, O you of little faith?

Hebrews 11:6 And without faith it is impossible to please him, for whoever would draw near to God must believe that he exists and that he rewards those who seek him.

Notes:

February 27th

Faith

Faith is the easy, restful, fearless attitude of an infant reposing on his mother's breast, with no thought of fear, effort or uncertainty.

Faith is not intellectual acceptance, blind credulity, naïve optimism, trying hard to believe, positive thinking, presumption. Faith is reasoning trust which never ignores reality.

Eph. 6:16 At all times carry faith as a shield; for with it you will be able to put out all the burning arrows shot by the Evil One. GNB.

Matthew 9:22 Jesus turned, and seeing her he said, "Take heart, daughter; your faith has made you well."

Hebrews 10:22 . . . let us draw near with a true heart in full assurance of faith, with our hearts sprinkled clean from an evil conscience and our bodies washed with pure water.

Notes:

Faith

Faith is like a muscle. The more you exercise, the bigger it grows.

Dr. Bill Bright

Faith is the venture of the whole personality in trusting one who is worthy. Faith is not really faith until it's all you're holding on to.

A faith which costs nothing, is worth nothing.

Gal. 2:20 I have been crucified with Christ. It is no longer I who live, but Christ who lives in me. And the life I now live in the flesh I live by faith in the Son of God, who loved me and gave himself for me.

2 Cor. 5:7 . . . for we walk by faith, not by sight.

Matthew 14:31 Jesus immediately reached out his hand and took hold of him (Peter), saying to him, "O you of little faith, why did you doubt?"

Notes:

February 29th

Faith

Faith is trusting God in the face of every fear, every doubt and every difficulty.

Faith anticipates, ventures, evaluates. It pays no attention to impossibilities and believes in miracles.

Faith never knows where it is being led, but it loves and knows the one who is leading. *Oswald Chambers*

Hebrews 11:1 To have faith is to be sure of the things we hope for, to be certain of the things we cannot see. GNB.

James 2:14, 26 What good is it, my brothers, if someone says he has faith but does not have works? Can that faith save him? . . . For as the body apart from the spirit is dead, so also faith apart from works is dead.

Romans 10:17 So faith comes from hearing, and hearing through the word of Christ.

Notes:

Faith

Faith is believing God's word to be true, even if we have no visible, tangible or audible proof that it is.

Doubt and fear are the enemies of faith.

Faith enables the believing soul to treat the future as present, and the invisible as seen. *Oswald Sanders*

The object of Christian faith is God.

Gal. 5:16 But I (Paul) say, walk by the Spirit, and you will not gratify the desires of the flesh.

2 Tim. 4:7 I have fought the good fight, I have finished the race, I have kept the faith.

1 Tim. 1:5 The purpose of this order is to arouse the love that comes from a pure heart, a clear conscience, and a genuine faith. GNB.

1 John 5:4 . . . And this is the victory that has overcome the world – our faith.

Notes:

March 2nd

Faith

Faith Asks Impossible Things Humbly.

No matter what the circumstances around us may be, faith gives us the assurance that God will prevail. No matter what the consequences before us, faith gives us the conviction that God will triumph. Faith gives us eyes to see and feet to stand on when everything around us threatens us and everything ahead of us looks like disaster.

Warren Wiersbe

Gal. 2:16 Yet we know that a person is put right with God only through faith in Jesus Christ, never by doing what the Law requires. GNB.

Matthew 17:20 He (Jesus) said to them (the disciples) . . . "For truly, I say to you, if you have faith like a grain of mustard seed, you will say to this mountain, 'Move from here to there', and it will move, and nothing will be impossible for you."

Notes:

Faith

When God has a gigantic task to be performed, faith gets the contract.

The profession of faith is not the same as the possession of faith.

Faith is to look at Earth from Heaven's point of view.

True faith is obeying God in spite of feelings, circumstances or consequences.

James 5:14,15 Are any of you ill? You should send for the church elders, who will pray for them and rub olive oil on them in the name of the Lord. This prayer made in faith will heal the sick; the Lord will restore them to health, and the sins they have committed will be forgiven. GNB.

Notes:

March 4th

Faith

Faith grows with the assault on it.

A faith not worth testing is not worth having.

Faith is simply taking God at His word, accepting what He asserts and acting accordingly.

Any faith that must be supported by the evidence of the senses is not real faith.

Hebrews 12:1,2 As for us, we have this large crowd of witnesses round us. So then, let us rid ourselves of everything that gets in the way, and of the sin which holds on to us so tightly, and let us run with determination the race that lies before us. Let us keep our eyes fixed on Jesus, on whom our faith depends from beginning to end. GNB.

Notes:

Faith

When I cannot enjoy the faith of assurance, I live by the faith of adherence. *Matthew Henry*

Faith is not asking for what we have not got, but making use of what God says we have.

Romans 12:3 And because of God's gracious gift to me (Paul) I say to every one of you: do not think of yourself more highly than you should. Instead, be modest in your thinking, and judge yourself according to the amount of faith that God has given you. GNB.

Habakkuk 2:4 . . . the righteous shall live by his faith.

Notes:

March 6th

Fear

The acid test of a true fear of the Lord is obedience.

It is not our love for Him that drives away fear, but His love for us.

Fear of God is a hatred of everything which is not of God.

Psalm: 111:10 The fear of the LORD is the beginning of wisdom; all those who practise it have a good understanding.

2 Cor. 7:1 Since we have these promises, beloved, let us cleanse ourselves from every defilement of body and spirit, bringing holiness to completion in the fear of God.

Notes:

Fear

Is fear knocking at your door right now? Then, as you answer its knocks, take Jesus with you. Don't be surprised to find no one there. *Selwyn Hughes*

Fear is an absence of love. God's love drives out fear.

Phil. 2:12 Therefore, my beloved, as you have always obeyed, so now, not only as in my (Paul) presence but much more in my absence, work our your own salvation with fear and trembling . . .

Psalm 2:11 Serve the LORD with fear, and rejoice with trembling.

Notes:

Fear

Fear is an awareness of the presence of the Lord. It dreads to disobey Him, but loves to serve him.

Fear is to revere His person and His authority, to delight in doing His will, while shunning all that is displeasing to Him.

---

1 John 4:18 There is no fear in love; perfect love drives out all fear. So then, love has not been made perfect in anyone who is afraid, because fear has to do with punishment. GNB.

Isaiah 41:10 fear not, for I (the LORD) am with you; be not dismayed, for I am your God;

Notes:

Fear

The fear of the Lord comes from a sense of God's holiness and His indignation against sin.

All fear is rooted in one thing – inner division.

There is nothing to fear, but fear.

---

2 Tim. 1:7 for God gave us a spirit not of fear but of power and love and self-control.

Deut. 10:12 And now, Israel, what does the Lord your God require of you, but to fear the LORD your God . . .

Notes:

March 10th

Fear

What do we have to do in order to be rid of fear?

1. Do not be afraid to admit it.
2. Give up all justification for your fears.
3. Fix it in your mind that to be controlled by fear is a fool's business.

Selwyn Hughes

(Continued tomorrow)

Isaiah 11:3 And his (the Messiah) delight shall be in the fear of the LORD.

Psalm 23:4 Even though I walk through the valley of the shadow of death, I will fear no evil, for you are with me;

Psalm 25:14 The friendship of the LORD is for those who fear him. . . .

Notes:

Fear

(Continued from yesterday)

4. Every fear you face has been defeated by Jesus.
5. Surrender all your fears into God's hand.
6. Repeat 1 John 4:18 – there is no fear in love; perfect love drives out all fear. GNB.

Selwyn Hughes

Fear is the enemy of faith.

Fear is love tinged with awe.

Matthew 10:28 Do not be afraid of those who kill the body but cannot kill the soul; rather be afraid of God, who can destroy both body and soul in hell. GNB.

Psalm 27:1 The LORD is my light and my salvation; whom shall I fear?

Notes:

March 12th

Fear

So the answer to your problem of fear lies not in self-centred efforts to conquer it, but in concentrating on the fact that God loves you, and has control of all the situations and circumstances of your life. The more you focus on that fact, the more His love will flow in, and the more fear will flow out. We are never afraid of those who love us.

Selwyn Hughes

Joshua 24:14 Now therefore fear the LORD and serve him in sincerity and in faithfulness.

Ecclesiastes 12:13 The end of the matter; all has been heard. Fear God and keep his commandments, for this is the whole duty of man.

Notes:

Feeling

Feeling is occupied with self; it looks inward and is discouraged. It is associated with ones own fluctuating condition. On the other hand, faith has to do with God and his eternal infallible word, his unchanging truth and Christ's eternal enduring sacrifice. Faith looks upward and is encouraged. *C. H. Spurgeon*

Eph. 4: 22,23,24 So get rid of your old self, which made you live as you used to – the old self that was being destroyed by its deceitful desires. Your hearts and minds must be made completely new, and you must put on the new self, which is created in God's likeness and reveals itself in the true life that is upright and holy. GNB.

Notes:

March 14th

Feeling

For feelings come and feelings go and feelings
are deceiving,
my warrant is the word of God, nought else is
worth believing.

Though all my heart should feel condemned for want
of some sweet token,
there is one greater than my heart whose word
cannot be broken.

I'll trust in God's unchanging word till soul and
body sever,
for though all things shall pass away, His word shall
stand forever.

Martin Luther

Col. 3:16 Let the word of Christ dwell in you richly . . .

Notes:

Fellowship

The only lasting fellowship between men, is the fellowship of sinners redeemed. *R. V. G. Tasker*

Seven practical commands to keep us in fellowship with God and one another.

1. Submit to God.
2. Resist the Devil (with the word of God).
3. Draw near to God.

Selwyn Hughes

(Continued tomorrow)

---

1 John 1: 6,7 If, then, we say that we have fellowship with him (God), yet at the same time live in the darkness, we are lying both in our words and in our actions. But if we live in the light – just as he is in the light – then we have fellowship with one another, and the blood of Jesus, his Son, purifies us from every sin. GNB.

Notes:

March 16th

Fellowship

(Continued from yesterday)

4. Cleanse and purify yourself.
5. Repent of known sin.
6. Humble yourself.
7. Don't speak evil of one another.

Selwyn Hughes

We need one another, otherwise we are like coal out of a fire.

---

1 Cor. 1:9 God is to be trusted, the God who called you to have fellowship with his Son Jesus Christ, our Lord. GNB

2 Cor. 13:14 The grace of the Lord Jesus Christ and the love of God and the fellowship of the Holy Spirit be with you all.

Notes:

Forgiveness

Forgiveness is an act of will in which a person relinquishes any right to get even with an offender.

Even where forgiveness is impossible (where there is no repentance on the other side), the desire and willingness to forgive must be there.

Matthew 18:21,22 Then Peter came up and said to him, "Lord, how often will my brother sin against me, and I forgive him? As many as seven times?" Jesus said to him, "I do not say to you seven times, but seventy times seven."

Psalm 25:18 Consider my affliction and my trouble, and forgive all my sins.

Notes:

March 18th

Forgiveness

Forgiveness is more than just surrendering my right to hurt you back. It is an extension of love and compassion toward an offending person.

Forgiveness is primarily a choice. It is a crisis of the will and the reward is freedom.

Forgiveness may be free, but it is never cheap.

Luke 23:34 And Jesus said, "Father, forgive them, for they know not what they do."

2 Chron. 7:14 . . . if my people who are called by my name humble themselves, and pray and seek my face and turn from their wicked ways, then I will hear from heaven and will forgive their sin and heal their land.

Notes:

Forgiveness

Forgiveness is the sense of freedom from resentment, bitterness and malice. It is giving up the right to hurt you for hurting me.

In asking for forgiveness, admit to guilt, state the offence and have a clear-cut request for forgiveness.

God offers forgiveness in a nail-pierced hand.

Matthew 18:34,35 And in anger his master delivered him to the jailers, until he should pay all his debt. So also my heavenly Father will do to every one of you, if you do not forgive your brother from your heart.

Acts 10:43 To him (Jesus) all the prophets bear witness that everyone who believes in him receives forgiveness of sins, through his name.

Notes:

March 20th

Forgiveness

Christians are not only forgiven, but they are also forgiving and for giving.

The Lord has assuredly a just cause for complaint against us because of our rebellion, and yet in free grace has extended His forgiveness. *D. A. Carson*

Forgiveness separates the offender from the offence – a definite act of the will.

Matthew 26:28 . . . for this is my blood of the covenant, which is poured out for many for the forgiveness of sins.

Eph. 1:7 In him (Jesus) we have redemption through his blood, the forgiveness of our trespasses, according to the riches of his grace . . .

1 John 2:12 I am writing to you, little children, because your sins are forgiven for his name's sake.

Notes:

Forgiveness

Sometimes the hardest person of all to forgive is the one in the mirror.

Only the truly forgiven are truly forgiving. We all agree that forgiveness is a beautiful idea, until we have to practise it.

C. S. Lewis

Christians are not perfect – just forgiven.

Col. 2:13 You were at one time spiritually dead because of your sins and because you were Gentiles without the Law. But God has now brought you to life with Christ. God forgave us all our sins; GNB.

Daniel 9:9 To the Lord our God belong mercy and forgiveness, for we have rebelled against him . . .

Hebrews 9:22 . . . and without the shedding of blood there is no forgiveness of sins.

Notes:

March 22nd

Forgiveness

Real forgiveness means looking steadfastly at the sin, the sin that is left over without any excuse after all allowances have been made, and seeing it in all its horror, dirt, meanness and malice, and nevertheless being wholly reconciled to the man who has done it. That, and only that, is forgiveness. *C. S. Lewis*

Mark 11:25 And whenever you stand praying, forgive, if you have anything against anyone, so that your Father also who is in heaven may forgive you your trespasses.

Psalm 86:5 For you, O Lord, are good and forgiving, abounding in steadfast love to all who call upon you.

Psalm 85:2 You have forgiven your people's sins and pardoned all their wrongs. GNB.

Notes:

Forgiveness

How do we go about it?

1. Don't minimise the offence.
2. Forgiveness is not an emotional thing, but an act of the will.
3. Forgiveness decides to relinquish any attempts at overt or covert retaliation.
4. Forgiveness can end the conflict, but lays the foundation to build a new relationship.

Selwyn Hughes

Matthew 6:14,15 For if you forgive others their trespasses, your heavenly Father will also forgive you, but if you do not forgive others their trespasses, neither will your Father forgive your trespasses.

1 John 1:9 If we confess our sins, he is faithful and just to forgive us our sins and to cleanse us from all unrighteousness.

Notes:

March 24th

Forgiveness

Forgiveness is a promise not to remember another's sin and never to again bring it up – not to him, not to others, not to yourself.

Feelings may or may not change at the time you forgive.

Col. 3:13 Be tolerant with one another and forgive one another whenever any of you has a complaint against someone else. You must forgive one another just as the Lord has forgiven you. GNB.

Psalm 103:12 as far as the east is from the west, so far does he remove our transgressions from us.

Notes:

Freedom

Freedom lies on the far side of obedience.

God created us for freedom in dependence on Himself, and man's truest freedom springs from his obedience to God.

Freedom is an inner contentment with what you have. It means to covet only heavenly treasure.

Gal. 5:13 For you were called to freedom, brothers. Only do not use your freedom as an opportunity for the flesh, but through love serve one another.

John 8:36 So if the Son sets you free, you will be free indeed.

Notes:

March 26th

Freedom

True Christian freedom is freedom to obey Christ, not to disobey Him. We are free not to do what we want, but to do what we ought.

Freedom is the by-product of obedience – obedience to Christ.

---

1 Peter 2:16 Live as people who are free, not using your freedom as a cover-up for evil, but living as servants of God.

2 Cor. 3:17 Now the Lord is the Spirit, and where the Spirit of the Lord is, there is freedom.

Notes:

Friends/Friendship

A friend is the one who comes in, when the whole world has gone out.

Friendship is the knitting of one soul with another, so that both become stronger and better by virtue of their relationship.

The best of friends are only friends at best.

John 15:15 No longer do I (Jesus) call you servants, for the servant does not know what his master is doing; but I have called you friends, for all that I have heard from my Father I have made known to you.

Proverbs 17:17 A friend loves at all times, and a brother is born for adversity.

Notes:

Friends/Friendship

Friendship is a single soul dwelling in two bodies.

A friend is someone who knows all there is to know about you and loves you just the same.

A true friend is someone who, when things are at their worst, they are at their best. *Bob Gass*

Friendship doubles our joy and divides our grief.

Proverbs 22:24 Make no friendship with a man given to anger . . .

James 4:4 . . . Do you not know that friendship with the world is enmity with God?

Proverbs 16:28 A dishonest man spreads strife, and a whisperer separates close friends.

John 15:14 You are my friends if you do what I (Jesus) command you.

Notes:

Giving

Make all you can, save all you can, give all you can.

John Wesley

The mind grows by "taking in", but the heart grows by "giving out".

If Jesus Christ be God and died for me, then no sacrifice can be too great for me to make for Him. *C. T. Studd*

1 Tim. 6:18 They (the rich) are to do good, to be rich in good works, to be generous and ready to share . . .

Isaiah 40:29 He gives power to the faint, and to him who has no might he increases strength.

2 Cor. 8:3 For they (the churches in Macedonia) gave according to their means, as I can testify, and beyond their means, of their own free will . . .

Notes:

March 30th

Giving

Some give like a sponge – only when they are squeezed.
Some give like Moses's rock – only when they are hit.
True Christians however give like the honeysuckle – because they delight to.

Charles Harthen

The significance of a life is not determined by its duration, but by its donation.

Deut. 16:17 Every man shall give as he is able, according to the blessing of the LORD your God that he has given you.

Matthew 7:11 If you then, who are evil, know how to give good gifts to your children, how much more will you father who is in heaven give good things to those who ask him!

Notes:

Giving

We can only fully receive from Christ when we fully give ourselves to Christ. *Martin Luther*

If we do not give according to our resources, then God will make our resources according to our giving.

God gives where he finds empty hands. *St. Augustine*

Generosity is giving with a warm hand.

Romans 8:32 He who did not spare his own Son but gave him up for us all, how will he not also with him graciously give us all things?

2 Cor. 9:7 Each one must give as he has made up his mind, not reluctantly or under compulsion, for God loves a cheerful giver.

Notes:

April 1st

Giving

The Lord measures giving, not by what we give, but what we keep for ourselves. *A. Cole*

Give as much of yourself as you know, to as much of Christ as you know.

He is not a fool who gives what he cannot keep to gain what he cannot lose. *Jim Elliot*

Luke 6:38 give, and it will be given to you. Good measure, pressed down, shaken together, running over, will be put into your lap.

1 Cor.12:7 To each is given the manifestation of the Spirit for the common good.

Matthew 7:7 Ask, and it will be given to you;

1 Cor. 15:57 But thanks be to God, who gives us the victory through our Lord Jesus Christ.

Notes:

Giving

Give me anything but thy frown, and anything with thy smile.

John Berridge

God is more interested in making us what we ought to be than in giving us what we think we ought to have.

We do not give anything to God until we give everything to God.

Nothing is really ours until we share it.

Proverbs 28:27 Whoever gives to the poor will not want . . .

1 Cor. 13:3 If I give away all I have, and if I deliver up my body to be burned, but have not love, I gain nothing.

Matthew 6:2,3 So when you give something to a needy person, do not make a big show of it, as the hypocrites do in the houses of worship and on the streets . . . But when you help a needy person, do it in such a way that even your closest friend will not know about it. GNB.

Notes:

April 3rd

Glory

Glory describes the revelation of the character and the presence of God in the person and work of Jesus Christ.

Our major goal in life is not to be happy or satisfied, but to glorify God.

God's glory will not only sustain you, but God's glory will also change you.

Psalm 19:1 The heavens declare the glory of God . . .

Psalm 57:11 Be exalted, O God, above the heavens! Let your glory be over all the earth!

1 Cor. 10:31 So, whether you eat or drink, or whatever you do, do all to the glory of God.

Matthew 25:31 When the Son of Man comes in his glory, and all the angels with him, then he will sit on his glorious throne.

Notes:

Godliness/Goodness

Godliness is God-like-ness

God-like character is both the fruit of the Spirit as He works within us and the result of our personal efforts. We are both totally dependent upon His working within us and totally responsible for our own character development.

Godliness is reverence towards God and respect towards men.

---

1 Tim. 4:7,8 Have nothing to do with irreverent, silly myths. Rather train yourself for godliness; for while bodily training is of some value, godliness is of value in every way . . .

Psalm 31:19 Oh, how abundant is your goodness, which you have stored up for those who fear you and worked for those who take refuge in you . . .

Notes:

April 5th

Godliness/Goodness

God is good to all in some ways and to some in all ways.

Godliness is devotion to God which results in a life that is pleasing to Him. *J. Bridges*

Goodness is the impression a Christian makes as he moves on his way blissfully unaware that he is reminding people of Jesus Christ.

---

1 Tim. 6:11 But as for you, O man of God, flee these things. Pursue righteousness, godliness, faith, love, steadfastness, gentleness.

Gal. 5:22 But the fruit of the Spirit is love, joy, peace, patience, kindness, goodness, faithfulness, gentleness, self-control;

2 Peter 3:11 Since all these things are thus to be dissolved, what sort of people ought you to be in lives of holiness and godliness . . .

Notes:

Grace

God's Riches At Christ's Expense

Grace is an act of forgiving, reconciling love.

Grace is goodwill, magnanimity and large heartedness. A Christian who has grace will have a generous disposition, will hold no bitterness and harbour no resentment. God only provides needed grace for needed moments.

---

1 Cor. 15:10 But by God's grace I am what I am, and the grace that he gave me was not without effect. GNB.

Titus 2:11 For God has revealed his grace for the salvation of the whole human race. GNB.

Eph. 2:8,9 For it is by God's grace that you have been saved through faith. It is not the result of your own efforts, but God's gift, so that no one can boast about it. GNB.

Notes:

April 7th

Grace

The grace of God is the soil in which a Christian develops and grows.

I cannot do everything, but I can do something. What I can do, I ought to do, and what I ought to do, by the Grace of God I will do. *Richard Baxter*

Grace is the favour of God.

Hebrews 4:16 Let us then with confidence draw near to the throne of grace, that we may receive mercy and find grace to help in time of need.

2 Peter 3:18 But grow in the grace and knowledge of our Lord and Saviour Jesus Christ.

2 Tim. 2:1 As for you, my son, be strong through the grace that is ours in union with Christ Jesus. GNB.

Notes:

Grace

Grace is getting what we do not deserve – God's forgiveness.

Grace is a word with a stoop in it. *D. L. Moody*

Strength in time of weariness,
Help in the hardest place,
Everything for nothing,
That, praise the Lord, is grace.

Romans 12:6 Having gifts that differ according to the grace given to us, let us use them:

James 4:6 But he (God) gives more grace. Therefore it (Scripture) says, "God opposes the proud, but gives grace to the humble."

Titus 3:6,7 God poured out the Holy Spirit abundantly on us through Jesus Christ our Saviour, so that by his grace we might be put right with God and come into possession of the eternal life we hope for. GNB.

Notes:

April 9th

Grace

Grace expresses two complementary thoughts; God's unmerited favour to us through Christ and God's divine assistance to us through the Holy Spirit.

The law means I do something for God, grace means God does something for me. *Watchman Nee*

Grace is God's love in action.

Romans 5:20 Law was introduced in order to increase wrongdoing; but where sin increased, God's grace increased much more. GNB.

1 Peter 1:13 Therefore, preparing your minds for action, and being sober-minded, set your hope fully on the grace that will be brought to you at the revelation of Jesus Christ.

Notes:

Grace

Grace is God with a face.

"What is grace?" I know until you ask me; when you ask me, I do not know. *St. Augustine*

Grace is the strength God gives us to live as His son lived when He was here upon earth. *Selwyn Hughes*

Eph. 2:4,5,6 But God's mercy is so abundant, and his love for us is so great, that while we were spiritually dead in our disobedience he brought us to life with Christ. It is by God's grace that you have been saved. In our union with Christ Jesus he raised us up with him to rule with him in the heavenly world. GNB.

Notes:

April 11th

Grace

Grace comes free of charge to people who do not deserve it. Grace does not depend on what we have done for God, but rather what God has done for us. *Philip Yancey*

Grace costs nothing for the recipient, but everything for the giver. Grace is free only because the giver himself has borne the cost.

Acts 4:33 And with great power the apostles were giving their testimony to the resurrection of the Lord Jesus, and great grace was upon them all.

1 Peter 5:5 Likewise, you who are younger, be subject to the elders. Clothe yourselves, all of you, with humility towards one another, for "God opposes the proud but gives grace to the humble."

Notes:

Grace

You are who you are because He is who He is.

Rejoice in what you are by the grace of God, rather than in the way God uses you.

Under the covenant of grace, sin is not only forgiven, but the sinner is enabled to overcome it. *Matthew Poole*

---

1 Peter 5:10 And after you have suffered for a little while, the God of all grace, who has called you to his eternal glory in Christ, will himself restore, confirm, strengthen and establish you.

Hebrews 2:9 But we do see Jesus, who for a little while was made lower than the angels, so that through God's grace he should die for everyone. GNB.

Notes:

April 13th

Grace

Imperfection is the prerequisite of grace. Light only gets in through cracks.

Grace is not a reward for the faithful, it is His gift for the empty, feeble, failing and undeserving. *Roy Hession*

He giveth more grace when the burdens grow greater. He sendeth more strength when the labours increase.

Hebrews 13:9 Do not be led away by diverse and strange teachings, for it is good for the heart to be strengthened by grace . . .

Eph. 1:4,5,6 Because of his love God had already decided that through Jesus Christ he would make us his sons and daughters – this was his pleasure and purpose. Let us praise God for his glorious grace, for the free gift he gave us in his dear Son! GNB.

Notes:

Grace

Grace gives, sin takes away.

Grace is God's kindness bestowed upon the undeserving; benevolence handed down to those who have no merit; a hand reaching down to those who have fallen into a pit. The Bible bids us believe that on the throne of the universe, there is a God like that. *Selwyn Hughes*

Eph. 4:7 But grace was given to each one of us according to the measure of Christ's gift.

1 Peter 4:10 As each has received a gift, use it to serve one another, as good stewards of God's varied grace:

Gal. 1:15 But God in his grace chose me (Paul) even before I was born, and called me to serve him. GNB.

Notes:

April 15th

Grace

Grace is love that is willing to pay a price.

Grace is love at its loveliest, falling on the unlovely and making it lovely.

Grace is the sole source from which flows the goodwill, love and salvation of God into His chosen people.

A. W. Pink

John 1:17 For the law was given through Moses; grace and truth came through Jesus Christ.

Romans 3:23,24 for all have sinned and fall short of the glory of God, and are justified by his grace as a gift, through the redemption that is in Christ Jesus . . .

2 Cor. 6:1 Working together with him, then, we appeal to you not to receive the grace of God in vain.

Notes:

Grace

Grace is love at work.

Grace is undeserved, unearnable, unrepayable.

It takes more grace than I can tell, to play the second fiddle well.

P. Hacking

Grace is the fully underserved favour of God towards sinners.

---

2 Cor. 12:7,8,9 But to keep me (Paul) from being puffed up with pride because of the many wonderful things I saw, I was given a painful physical ailment . . . Three times I prayed to the Lord about this and asked him to take it away. But his answer was: "My grace is all you need, for my power is greatest when you are weak." GNB.

Notes:

April 17th

Grace

Grace's purpose is to restore man's relationship with God.

Grace means there is nothing we can do to make God love us more and grace means there is nothing we can do to make God love us less.

Grace is the strength God gives us to obey commands.

Hebrews 12:15 See to it that no one fails to obtain the grace of God;

Romans 5:2 Through him we have also obtained access by faith into this grace in which we stand, and we rejoice in hope of the glory of God.

John 1:14 And the Word became flesh and dwelt among us, and we have seen his glory, glory as of the only Son from the Father, full of grace and truth.

Notes:

Grace

We need grace to purify our souls.

Grace is love applied; favouring us when we are not favourable, loving us when we are not loveable, accepting us when we are not acceptable, redeeming us when by all the laws of the universe we do not deserve it.

Romans 6:14 Sin must not be your master; for you do not live under law but under God's grace. GNB.

2 Cor. 8:9 For you know the grace of our Lord Jesus Christ, that though he was rich, yet for your sake he became poor, so that you by his poverty might become rich.

2 Thess. 3:18 The grace of our Lord Jesus Christ be with you all.

Notes:

April 19th

Guidance

Our need to be guided is often greater than our willingness.

God wants to guide us, not override us.

In order to get guidance in a crisis, remain in the will of God in the continuous.

The first duty of every soul is to find not its freedom, but its Master. *Peter Forsythe*

Psalm 32:8 I will instruct you and teach you in the way you should go;

Deut. 8:2 And you shall remember the whole way that the LORD your God has led you these forty years in the wilderness, that he might humble you, testing you to know what was in your heart, whether you would keep his commandments or not.

Notes:

Guidance

God's guidance comes in response to our active obedience, not in response to our passive waiting.

It is comforting to know that not only the steps but also the stops of a good person are ordered by the Lord.

George Müller

Psalm 23:3 He restores my soul. He leads me in the paths of righteousness for his name's sake.

Psalm 119:105 Your word is a lamp to guide me and a light for my path. GNB.

Proverbs 11:14 A nation will fall if it has no guidance. GNB.

Notes:

April 21st

Guidance

God sometimes puts His children to bed in the dark.

General routes to guidance.

1. Guidance according to the character of Christ.
2. Guidance through His word.
3. Guidance through circumstances.
4. Guidance through the counsel of good and godly people.
5. Guidance through the direct whispering of the Spirit within us.

Selwyn Hughes

Isaiah 30:21 And your ears shall hear a word behind you, saying, "This is the way, walk in it", when you turn to the right or when you turn to the left.

Psalm 27:11 Teach me your way, O LORD, and lead me on a level path because of my enemies.

Notes:

Guidance

God's guidance is always sufficiently obvious to be found, but not so obvious that it does away with the necessity of thought and discriminating insight. *E. Stanley Jones*

Whenever God's finger points the way to anything, His hand always provides the power.

God prepares us for what He has prepared for us.

Exodus 15:13 You have led in your steadfast love the people whom you have redeemed; you have guided them by your strength to your holy abode.

James 4:17 So whoever knows the right thing to do and fails to do it, for him it is sin.

Notes:

April 23rd

Guidance

Often things don't go our way because they are going His way.

Where God guides He provides; where He directs He protects. *Bob Gass*

God wants us to be independently dependent.

In seeking guidance, obedience to the light already given is essential.

Expect great things from God, attempt great things for God. *William Carey*

Proverbs 12:26 One who is righteous is a guide to his neighbour . . .

Isaiah 58:11 And I (the LORD) will always guide you and satisfy you with good things. GNB.

Romans 8:28 And we know that for those who love God all things work together for good, for those who are called according to his purpose.

Notes:

Guidance

I have lived, seen God's hand through a lifetime, and all was for the best.
R. Browning

We see a horizon, but God often works beyond it.

His guidance will not cripple our initiative.

If you're heading in the wrong direction, God allows U-turns.

Luke 24:50 Then he (Jesus) led them out as far as Bethany, and lifting up his hands he blessed them.

Genesis 24:27 . . . As for me, the LORD has led me in the way to the house of my master's kinsmen.

Psalm 78:52 Then he led out his people like sheep and guided them in the wilderness like a flock.

Notes:

April 25th

Guidance

God never takes away the good, unless He plans to replace it with the better.

Our grand business is not to see what lies dimly in the distance, but to do what lies clearly to hand. *T. Carlyle*

God will not issue further instructions beyond our last act of disobedience.

Psalm 139:9,10 If I take the wings of the morning and dwell in the uttermost parts of the sea, even there your hand shall lead me, and your right hand shall hold me.

Luke 4:1 And Jesus, full of the Holy Spirit, returned from the Jordan and was led by the Spirit in the wilderness for forty days, being tempted by the devil.

Notes:

Guidance

Before a door can be opened, it must be closed.

He will prepare us for what He is preparing for us.

In the light of eternity we shall see that what we desired would have been fatal to us, and that which we would have avoided is essential to our well-being. *Fenelon*

Mark 13:11 And when they bring you to trial and deliver you over, do not be anxious beforehand what you are to say, but say whatever is given you in that hour, for it is not you who speak, but the Holy Spirit.

Romans 8:14 For all who are led by the Spirit of God are sons of God.

Notes:

April 27th

Guidance

God doesn't call extraordinary people to do extraordinary things. He calls ordinary people to do ordinary things in an extraordinary way.

There are no short-cuts (to guidance) on a straight road.

That which we took hold of in the light, do not let go in the dark.

John 16:13 When the Spirit of truth comes, he will guide you into all the truth, for he will not speak on his own authority, but whatever he hears he will speak, and he will declare to you the things that are to come.

Psalm 73:24 You guide me with your counsel, and afterwards you will receive me to glory.

Notes:

Guilt

Guilt is God's way of saying – "you have broken one of my principles".

Bill Gothard

Real guilt is the result of violating one of God's principles. False guilt is produced when you violate one of your own principles.

Guilt lies in cherishing and retaining the desire.

Psalm 25:11 For your name's sake, O LORD, pardon my guilt, for it is great.

Isaiah 6:7 And he (the seraphim) touched my mouth and said: "Behold, this (a burning coal) has touched your lips; your guilt is taken away, and your sin atoned for."

Acts 13:28 And though they found in him (Jesus) no guilt worthy of death, they asked Pilate to have him executed.

Notes:

April 29th

Happiness

Happiness is not what we have, but whatever we are thankful for.

No one will ever find true happiness, except in relation to abiding in the will of God. *C. S. Lewis*

The pursuit of holiness results in joy and happiness.

Contentment isn't getting what we want, but enjoying what we've got.

Luke 6:22,23 Blessed are you when people hate you and when they exclude you and revile you and spurn your name as evil, on account of the Son of Man! Rejoice in that day . . .

Psalm 119:35 Keep me obedient to your commandments, because in them I find happiness. GNB.

Psalm 40:4 Happy are those who trust the LORD . . . GNB.

Notes:

Happiness

True happiness is selfless love of others.

The Christian's ultimate goal in life is not to be happy, but to glorify God.
C. Swindoll

Happiness is a by-product of service, never a result.

One way to find happiness is to renounce your right to it.

You cannot make happiness, it is something you receive.

Luke 6:20,21 And he (Jesus) lifted up his eyes on his disciples, and said: "Blessed (happy) are you who are poor, for yours is the kingdom of God. Blessed are you who are hungry now, for you shall be satisfied."

Proverbs 28:14 Always obey the LORD and you will be happy. GNB.

Notes:

May 1st

Happiness

Until we recognise that life is not just something to be enjoyed, but rather is a task that each of us is assigned, we will never find meaning in our lives, and will never be truly happy. *Dr. V. Frankl*

The end of life is not happiness, but growth in character and spiritual achievement.

Isaiah 61:10 I will greatly rejoice in the LORD; my soul shall exult in my God . . .

James 1:12 Blessed is the man who remains steadfast under trial, for when he has stood the test he will receive the crown of life, which God has promised to those who love him.

Notes:

Heaven

Those who get to Heaven will not regret for one moment what they abandoned here on Earth. *Selwyn Hughes*

There is life in the hereafter, and the quality of life in the hereafter depends on what you are after here.

Heaven is that which is above.

Matthew 6:9 Pray then like this: "Our Father in heaven, hallowed be your name."

Psalm 123:1 To you I lift up my eyes, O you who are enthroned in the heavens!

John 3:27 . . . A person cannot receive even one thing unless it is given him from heaven.

Matthew 24:35 Heaven and earth will pass away, but my words will not pass away.

Notes:

May 3rd

Heaven

Heaven is the place where God is.

Heaven has the best architect, the best site, and the longest possible lease.

Aim at Heaven and you will get Earth thrown in; aim at Earth and you will get neither. *C. S. Lewis*

Matthew 6:19,20 Do not lay up for yourselves treasures on earth . . . but lay up for yourselves treasures in heaven . . .

Matthew 28:18 And Jesus came and said to them (the disciples), "All authority in heaven and on earth has been given to me."

Notes:

Heaven

If we insist on holding onto sinful ways, then we shall not see Heaven.
Selwyn Hughes

Some people may miss Heaven by eighteen inches, the distance from their head to their heart (do you really know Christ or only about him).

Matthew 7:21 Not everyone who says to me, "Lord, Lord", will enter the kingdom of heaven, but the one who does the will of my Father who is in heaven.

Isaiah 66:1 Thus says the LORD: "Heaven is my throne, and the earth is my footstool;"

Phil. 3:20 But our citizenship is in heaven, and from it we await a Saviour, the Lord Jesus Christ . . .

Notes:

May 5th

Holiness

Holiness is leaving behind that which is evil, and leaning to that which is good.

Holiness is not a destination, but a journey.

A holy person is one who is sanctified by the presence and action of God in them.

There are no short cuts to holiness.

Exodus 15:11 Who is like you, O LORD, among the gods? Who is like you, majestic in holiness, awesome in glorious deeds, doing wonders?

1 Thess. 4:7 God did not call us to live in immorality, but in holiness. GNB.

Hebrews 12:14 Strive for peace with everyone, and for the holiness without which no one will see the Lord.

Notes:

Holy Spirit

The Greek term for the Holy Spirit is *parakletos*: the literal meaning is "one who comes alongside to help". Variously translated into English as the words counsellor, helper, comforter.

The Holy Spirit is the One who makes real in you all that Jesus did for you. *Oswald Chambers*

John 14:26 But the Helper, the Holy Spirit, whom the Father will send in my (Jesus's) name, he will teach you all things and bring to your remembrance all that I have said to you.

Acts 2:4 And they were all filled with the Holy Spirit and began to speak in other tongues as the Spirit gave them utterance.

Notes:

May 7th

Holy Spirit

Whenever the Spirit is at work, change is inevitable.
Jay Adams

The Spirit is like electricity. He won't come in unless He can get out. *Billy Graham*

Thank God it is gloriously and majestically true that the Holy Spirit can work in us the very nature of Jesus, if we will obey Him. *Oswald Chambers*

Romans 8:13 For if you live according to the flesh you will die, but if by the Spirit you put to death the deeds of the body, you will live.

2 Cor. 3:17 Now the Lord is the Spirit, and where the Spirit of the Lord is, there is freedom.

Notes:

Holy Spirit

Characteristics of the Holy Spirit:

1. He seeks to draw out of us all the potential which God has built into us and is continually at work developing us into the kind of person God sees us to be.
2. He brings hidden things to light in our souls and seeks to rid us of all sin.

Selwyn Hughes

(Continued tomorrow)

Gal. 5:16 But I (Paul) say, walk by the Spirit, and you will not gratify the desires of the flesh.

John 15:26 But when the Helper comes, whom I (Jesus) will send to you from the Father, the Spirit of truth, who proceeds from the Father, he will bear witness about me.

Notes:

May 9th

Holy Spirit

(Continued from yesterday)

3. He shines the laser beam of knowledge and wisdom through the fog that sometimes surrounds us, and guides us in ways of which we are both conscious and unconscious along the path He wants us to take.
4. He teaches us as no other could teach us and leads us into the thing our hearts were built for – truth.

Selwyn Hughes

(Continued tomorrow)

Joel 2:28 And it shall come to pass afterwards, that I will pour out my Spirit on all flesh; your sons and your daughters shall prophesy, your old men shall dream dreams, and your young men shall see visions.

1 Cor. 3:16 Do you not know that you are God's temple and that God's Spirit dwells in you?

Notes:

Holy Spirit

(Continued from yesterday)

5. He prods us to prayer and on those occasions when we don't know how to pray as we ought, He takes over and prays in us and through us.
6. He comforts us whenever we are in need of solace and strengthens our hearts to go on even though we have no clear answers to our predicament.

Selwyn Hughes

Acts 1:8 But you will receive power when the Holy Spirit has come upon you, and you will be my witnesses . . .

Romans 8:11 If the Spirit of him who raised Jesus from the dead dwells in you, he who raised Christ Jesus from the dead will also give life to your mortal bodies, through his Spirit who dwells in you.

Notes:

Holy Spirit

The Holy Spirit provides the cutting edge for all Christian service.

The Holy Spirit wants to be more than resident. He wants to be president.

The Holy Spirit is God in action.

Luke 11:13 If you then, who are evil, know how to give good gifts to your children, how much more will the heavenly Father give the Holy Spirit to those who ask him!

1 Cor. 6:19 Don't you know that your body is the temple of the Holy Spirit, who lives in you and who was given to you by God? GNB.

Notes:

Holy spirit

Christ's work on the cross was for us, on our behalf; it affects only our status. The Spirit's work is within us and does something to us. It affects our state.

> All Spirit and no Word, you blow up.
> All Word and no Spirit, you dry up.

Donald Gee

Romans 8:16 God's Spirit joins himself to our spirits to declare that we are God's children. GNB.

Romans 8:26 Likewise the Spirit helps us in our weakness. For we do not know what to pray for as we ought, but the Spirit himself intercedes for us with groanings too deep for words.

1 Thess. 5:19 Do not quench the Spirit.

Notes:

May 13th

Hope

Hope is a conviction that, no matter what, love (agape love) will ultimately bring all things to a good and glorious end.

Hope in the Bible is not "hope so" – our hope is a certainty.

Hope is a sure and certain expectation with no shadow of doubt, no trace of disbelief.

Psalm 39:7 What, then, can I hope for, Lord? I put my hope in you. GNB.

Romans 12:12 Rejoice in hope, be patient in tribulation, be constant in prayer.

Romans 15:13 May the God of hope fill you with all joy and peace in believing, so that by the power of the Holy Spirit you may abound in hope.

Notes:

Hope

Hope is no other than the expectation of those things which faith has believed to be truly promised by God.

John Calvin

Hope is trusting God to act in His good timing.

Hope, in a worldly sense, is optimism.

Hope is the daughter of faith.

Hebrews 10:23 Let us hold on firmly to the hope we profess, because we can trust God to keep his promise. GNB.

Romans 15:4 For whatever was written in former days was written for our instruction, that through endurance and through the encouragement of the Scriptures we might have hope.

Notes:

May 15th

Hope

The Lord Himself is the source of hope, because He determines our future.

In the Bible, hope means to desire some good, with the expectation of obtaining it.

Life with Christ is an endless hope; without Him it is a hopeless end.

---

1 Peter 1:21 Through him (Jesus) you believe in God, who raised him from death and gave him glory; and so your faith and hope are fixed on God. GNB.

Romans 5:3,4,5 We also boast of our troubles, because we know that trouble produces endurance, endurance brings God's approval, and his approval creates hope. This hope does not disappoint us . . . GNB.

Notes:

Hope

The children of this world have their all in hand, and nothing in hope, while the children of God have their all in hope, and next to nothing in hand. *Matthew Henry*

Biblical hope is inseparable from faith in God.

---

1 Tim. 4:10 We struggle and work hard, because we have placed our hope in the living God . . . GNB.

Psalm 71:14 But I will hope continually and will praise you yet more and more.

Jeremiah 29:11 For I know the plans I have for you, declares the LORD, plans for wholeness and not for evil, to give you a future and a hope.

Notes:

May 17th

Humility

You don't find God through climbing a ladder of self-effort to find Him at the topmost rung. You find Him at the bottom of the ladder where He came down to us through His incarnation.

Don't confuse humility with inferiority.

Matthew 18:4 Whoever humbles himself like this child is the greatest in the kingdom of heaven.

Micah 6:8 . . . the LORD has told us what is good. What he requires of us is this: to do what is just, to show constant love, and to live in humble fellowship with our God. GNB.

Psalm 25:9 He leads the humble in what is right, and teaches the humble his way.

Notes:

Humility

If God and I disagree, I ask Him to change my mind.

Humility is the proper estimate of oneself.

C. H. Spurgeon

Biblically, humility is the attitude of mind that regards the interests of others as more important than one's own.

Phil. 2:8 And being found in human form, he (Jesus) humbled himself by becoming obedient to the point of death, even death on a cross.

Zechariah 9:9 . . . Look, your king is coming to you! He comes triumphant and victorious, but humble and riding on a donkey. GNB.

1 Peter 5:6 Humble yourselves, therefore, under the mighty hand of God so that at the proper time he may exalt you . . .

Notes:

May 19th

Humility

The true way to be humble is not to stoop until you are smaller than yourself, but to stand at your real height against some higher nature (Jesus) that will show you what the real smallness of your greatness is. *Philip Brookes*

Humility is always a choice.

Matthew 23:12 Whoever exalts himself will be humbled, and whoever humbles himself will be exalted.

1 Peter 5:5 . . . Clothe yourselves, all of you, with humility towards one another, for God opposes the proud but gives grace to the humble.

Notes:

Humility

If you ask me what is the first precept of the Christian religion, I will answer first, second and third – humility.

St. Augustine

It's wonderful what God can do with a broken heart if He is given all the pieces.

James 4:10 Humble yourselves before the Lord, and he will exalt you.

Proverbs 15:33 Reverence for the LORD is an education in itself. You must be humble before you can ever receive honours. GNB.

1 Peter 3:8 Finally, all of you, have unity of mind, sympathy, brotherly love, a tender heart, and a humble mind.

Notes:

May 21st

Humility

Humility is a true and absorbing view of oneself as seen from God's point of view.

In God's kingdom, the way up is the way down.

Humility is always the first step to God's grace and power.

Col. 3:12 Put on then, as God's chosen ones, holy and beloved, compassion, kindness, humility, meekness, and patience . . .

Proverbs 18:12 No one is respected unless he is humble; GNB.

Phil. 2:3 Do nothing from rivalry or conceit, but in humility count others more significant than yourselves.

Notes:

Idol/Idolatry

Idolatry is quite simply substituting one thing for another.

God is not against us owning things, what He is against is when we allow them to own us.

One idol cherished in the heart may ruin a soul for ever.

J. C. Ryle

Idolatry is probably the biggest hindrance to knowing God.

Exodus 20:3 You shall have no other gods before me.

1 Thess. 1:9 All those people speak about how you received us when we visited you, and how you turned away from idols to God . . . GNB.

Notes:

May 23rd

Idol/Idolatry

Idolatry can take many forms – self, possessions, people – anything that we give greater love and attention than God.

An idol is something relative that becomes absolute.

Idolatry is trusting anything other than the Lord for salvation.

Idolatry is the substitution of what is created, for the creator.

---

1 Cor. 10:14 Therefore, my beloved, flee from idolatry.

Jonah 2:8 Those who worship worthless idols have abandoned their loyalty to you (God). GNB.

Eph. 5:5 For you may be sure of this, that everyone who is sexually immoral or impure, or who is covetous (that is, an idolater), has no inheritance in the kingdom of Christ and God.

1 John 5:21 Little children, keep yourselves from idols.

Notes:

Integrity

Integrity is a commitment to do what is right regardless of the cost. It is being governed by settled convictions instead of momentary expediency. By principles rather than pragmatism. By vision rather than comfort, by mission rather than politics. By God's will rather than human will, for God's kingdom rather than our own. *John Wagner*

Proverbs 10:9 Whoever walks in integrity walks securely . . .

Proverbs 11:3 The integrity of the upright guides them . . .

Titus 2:7 Show yourself in all respects to be a model of good works, and in your teaching show integrity . . .

Notes:

May 25th

Jealousy

Jealousy is the hurt you feel when someone you regard as an equal or even superior, has surpassed you or is considered to have surpassed you. *Selwyn Hughes*

At the root of jealousy is rebellion, lack of trust, hard-heartedness, spiritual blindness, a wrong comparison with others.

Deut. 4:24 For the LORD your God is a consuming fire, a jealous God.

1 Kings 14:22 And Judah did what was evil in the sight of the LORD, and they provoked him to jealousy with their sins that they committed, more than all that their fathers had done.

Notes:

Jealousy

Jealousy is the pain, grief, annoyance felt at the happiness, success or fortune of another; displeasure or regret aroused by the superiority of another, plus a certain degree of malice or malignity and a desire to deprecate the person envied. *W. E. Sangster*

---

1 Cor. 3:3 . . . When there is jealousy among you and you quarrel with one another, doesn't this prove that you belong to this world, living by its standards? GNB.

Ezekiel 39:25 "Therefore thus says the Lord GOD: Now I will restore the fortunes of Jacob and have mercy on the whole house of Israel, and I will be jealous for my holy name."

Notes:

May 27th

Jealousy

Jealousy puts mirrors instead of windows in our hearts, so that we only see ourselves and what we are losing.

Jealousy is the pain of losing what I have to someone else, in spite of my efforts to keep it. *Charles Swindoll*

Gal. 5:19,20,21 Now the works of the flesh are evident: sexual immorality, impurity, sensuality, idolatry, sorcery, enmity, strife, jealousy . . . those who do such things will not inherit the kingdom of God.

Deut. 32:21 With their idols they have made me angry, jealous with their so-called gods, gods that are really not gods. GNB.

Notes:

Jealousy

Jealousy is a vice which takes no pleasure in itself.

Chaucer

Jealousy brings decay to our lives because it causes us to focus on anger and bitterness.

A jealous person is self-centred.

Proverbs 6:34 For jealousy makes a man furious, and he will not spare when he takes revenge.

Nahum 1:2 The LORD is a jealous and avenging God; the Lord is avenging and wrathful;

Exodus 20:5 You shall not bow down to them (images) or serve them, for I the LORD your God am a jealous God . . .

Notes:

May 29th

Jealousy

Jealousy is a secret elation we feel when someone we dislike stumbles and falls. Jealousy is deadly in its nature and it never fails to scar and scorch the soul. *Selwyn Hughes*

We are rarely jealous of the people we do not know, jealousy is focussed on those we know, those who are closest to us.

---

2 Cor. 11:2 I (Paul) am jealous for you, just as God is; you are like a pure virgin whom I have promised in marriage to one man only, Christ himself. GNB.

Proverbs 27:4 Wrath is cruel, anger is overwhelming, but who can stand before jealousy?

Notes:

Jesus Christ

Something awful happened to Christ, so that something wonderful might happen to us.

If I was asked to put the formula for victorious living into one sentence it would be this: To be a conqueror in Christ means first and foremost to be conquered by Christ.

Selwyn Hughes

Jesus is all, or nothing at all.

Isaiah 9:6 For to us a child is born, to us a son is given; and the government shall be upon his shoulder, and his name shall be called Wonderful Counsellor, Mighty God, Everlasting Father, Prince of Peace.

Romans 10:9 . . . if you confess with your mouth that Jesus is Lord and believe in your heart that God raised him from the dead, you will be saved.

Notes:

May 31st

Jesus Christ

Jesus puts the hand of a penitent sinner into the hand of a pardoning God.

Jesus is the heart of God wrapped in human flesh.

Jesus is good news, all else is good views.

The world has been honoured by a visit from its creator.

Luke 9:35 And a voice came out of the cloud, saying, "This is my Son, my Chosen One; listen to him!"

Hebrews 4:14 Let us, then, hold firmly to the faith we profess. For we have a great High Priest who has gone into the very presence of God – Jesus, the Son of God. GNB.

John 14:6 Jesus said to him (Thomas), "I am the way, and the truth, and the life. No one comes to the Father except through me."

Notes:

Jesus Christ

The Son of God (Jesus) became the Son of Man, that the sons of men might become the sons of God.

Jesus Exactly Suits Us Sinners.

Our real greatness in this world arises, not so much from what we do, but from whether or not we are directly related to Christ.

Hebrews 13:8 Jesus Christ is the same yesterday and today and for ever.

2 Cor. 5:17 Therefore, if anyone is in Christ, he is a new creation. The old has passed away; behold, the new has come.

Hebrews 7:26 Jesus, then, is the High Priest that meets our needs. He is holy; he has no fault or sin in him; he has been set apart from sinners and raised above the heavens. GNB.

Notes:

June 2nd

Joy

Joy is peace with its hat thrown high in the air and peace is joy with its arms folded in serenic assurance.

The joy that Christ gives is always there, supporting and strengthening you so that you can carry on.

Selwyn Hughes

Joy does not exclude weeping.

Proverbs 12:20 Deceit is in the heart of those who devise evil, but those who plan peace have joy.

Psalm 119:111 Your commandments are my eternal possession; they are the joy of my heart. GNB.

Phil. 2:2 . . . complete my (Paul) joy by being of the same mind, having the same love, being in full accord and of one mind.

Notes:

Joy

It is a blessed mark of growth out of spiritual infancy when we can forego the joys which once appeared to be essential and can find solace in Him who denies them to us.

C. H. Spurgeon

Joy is a deep abiding inner thankfulness and gratitude to God which is not interrupted when undesirable life circumstances intrude.

John 16:24 Until now you have asked nothing in my name. Ask, and you will receive, that your joy may be full.

Romans 15:13 May God, the source of hope, fill you with all joy and peace by means of your faith in him, so that your hope will continue to grow by the power of the Holy Spirit. GNB.

Gal. 5:22 But the fruit of the Spirit is . . . joy . . .

Notes:

June 4th

Joy

Christianity is the most joyous, the least forbidding of all the religions of mankind. There is no religion which throws off the burden of life so completely, which escapes so swiftly from its moods, which gives so large a scope for the high spirits of the soul and welcomes to its bosom with so warm an embrace those things of beauty which are joys forever. *L. P. Jack*

Hebrews 12:2 Let us keep our eyes fixed on Jesus, on whom our faith depends from beginning to end. He did not give up because of the cross! On the contrary, because of the joy that was waiting for him, he thought nothing of the disgrace of dying on the cross . . . GNB.

James 1:2 Count it all joy, my brothers, when you meet trials of various kinds . . .

Notes:

Joy

Lack of joy is caused almost entirely through inner conflicts and wrong attitudes.

The joy of Jesus was the absolute self-surrender and self-sacrifice of Himself to His Father, the joy of doing that which the Father sent Him to do. *Oswald Chambers*

Psalm 81:1 Sing aloud to God our strength; shout for joy to the God of Jacob!

Matthew 13:44 "The kingdom of heaven is like treasure hidden in a field, which a man found and covered up. Then in his joy he goes and sells all that he has and buys that field."

Notes:

June 6th

Joy

Joy is the strength of the people of God; it is their glory, it is their characteristic mark. When the mark is absent, then the characteristics of a Christian are absent.

Joy is life in excess – the overflow of what cannot be contained within one person. *Eugene Peterson*

Psalm 16:11 You (God) will show me the path that leads to life; your presence fills me with joy and brings me pleasure for ever. GNB.

Luke 2:10 And the angel said to them (the shepherds), "Fear not, for behold, I bring you good news of a great joy that will be for all the people."

Notes:

Joy

Christ possesses joy in all its fullness and when we live in Him, He then gives it to us.

Joy is that deep abiding sense that all is well, even when circumstances are against us.

Joy is the by-product of obedience to God.

Acts 13:52 And the disciples were filled with joy and with the Holy Spirit.

Matthew 25:21 His master said to him, "Well done, good and faithful servant. You have been faithful over a little; I will set you over much. Enter into the joy of your master."

Nehemiah 8:10 . . . for the joy of the LORD is your strength.

Notes:

June 8th

Joy

Christian joy arises from the sense of sins forgiven and from the assurance that the sinner now enjoys the favour of God. *R. V. G. Tasker*

Joy is the flag flying high from the castle of my heart when the King is in residence there.

Isaiah 35:10 And the ransomed of the LORD shall return and come to Zion with singing; everlasting joy shall be upon their heads; they shall obtain gladness and joy, and sorrow and sighing shall flee away.

3 John 4 I (John) have no greater joy than to hear that my children are walking in the truth.

Notes:

Joy

The joyous Christian is the one who delights in God, rather than in what God provides.

If you have no joy in your religion, there's a leak somewhere in your Christianity. *Billy Sunday*

The formula for joy is quite simple – walk hand in hand with Jesus.

Psalm 43:4 Then I will go to the altar of God, to God my exceeding joy, and I will praise you with the lyre, O God, my God.

Romans 14:17 For the kingdom of God is not a matter of eating and drinking but of righteousness and peace and joy in the Holy Spirit.

Notes:

June 10th

Judgement

We should be slow to judge others, because only God can judge correctly every time.

Judgement delayed is not judgement denied.

God's judgements are often silent.

The judgements of God are an expression of His love.

Matthew 7:1,2 "Do not judge others, so that God will not judge you, for God will judge you in the same way as you judge others . . ." GNB.

Romans 14:10 . . . For we will all stand before the judgement seat of God;

1 Peter 4:17 The time has come for judgement to begin, and God's own people are the first to be judged. GNB.

Notes:

Justification

Justification means to declare to be righteous.

By the supernatural miracle of God's grace, I stand justified, not because I am sorry for my sin, not because I have repented, but because of what Jesus has done.

Oswald Chambers

Justification is God's forgiveness of the past, together with His acceptance for the future.

Gal. 3:11 Now it is evident that no one is justified before God by the law, for "The righteous shall live by faith."

1 Cor. 6:11 And such were some of you. But you were washed, you were sanctified, you were justified in the name of the Lord Jesus Christ and by the Spirit of our God.

Notes:

Justification

Justification is an act of God, by which He deals with the guilt of sin. He does this by imputing righteousness to the sinner who believes in Christ.

Justification is to be set right with God: accepted, acquitted, reinstated.

God credits sinners with Christ's legal and moral perfection.

A sinner is justified by being accounted as righteous.

Romans 3:23,24 . . . for all have sinned and fall short of the glory of God, and are justified by his grace as a gift, through the redemption that is in Christ Jesus . . .

Gal. 2:16 . . . yet we know that a person is not justified by works of the law but through faith in Jesus Christ . . .

Notes:

Justification

Justification is . . .

- the act of God when he pardons sinners and accepts them as righteous in His sight, because of Christ's perfect obedience and perfect sacrifice.
- not to make righteous, but account righteous.
- a legal term that speaks of our standing before God.
- a finished work.

Romans 3:20 For no one is put right in God's sight by doing what the Law requires; what the Law does is to make people know that they have sinned. GNB.

Titus 3:6,7 God poured out the Holy Spirit abundantly on us through Jesus Christ our Saviour, so that by his grace we might be put right with God and come into possession of the eternal life we hope for. GNB.

Romans 5:1 Therefore, since we have been justified by faith, we have peace with God through our Lord Jesus Christ.

Notes:

June 14th

Knowledge

Knowledge is the capacity to comprehend and retain what one is taught. Wisdom is the ability to put that knowledge to the best effect.

There is no true knowledge of God without the worship of God. *J. Calvin*

We will know God to the extent that we are willing to put His demands into practice, and no more.

Dr. Cyndyllan Jones

Proverbs 9:10 The fear of the LORD is the beginning of wisdom, and the knowledge of the Holy One is insight.

Romans 11:33 Oh, the depth of the riches and wisdom and knowledge of God!

2 Peter 3:18 But grow in the grace and knowledge of our Lord and Saviour Jesus Christ.

Notes:

Law

The law is to awaken a realisation of sin, but is incapable of removing it.

The law consists of our duty towards God, and our duty towards our neighbour.

We do not need the external Law of Moses to guide us, for the Law of God is written in our hearts.

Psalm 19:7 The law of the LORD is perfect; it gives new strength. GNB.

Psalm 119:18 Open my eyes, that I may behold wondrous things out of your law.

John 1:17 For the law was given through Moses; grace and truth came through Jesus Christ.

Gal. 5:14 For the whole law is fulfilled in one word: "You shall love your neighbour as yourself."

Notes:

June 16th

Life

Life is real and earnest and the grave is not its goal.

H. W. Longfellow

Life has to be lived forwards, but it can only be understood backwards.

Life is borrowed, transitory, dependent upon and at the disposal of God.

John 14:6 Jesus said to him (Thomas), "I am the way, and the truth, and the life. No one comes to the Father except through me."

John 17:3 And this is eternal life, that they know you the only true God, and Jesus Christ whom you have sent.

Notes:

Loneliness

Loneliness is a feeling of being bereft of human companionship. The sadness that comes through the loss of a loved one or the failure to find a close and loving friend. It is a sense of isolation, of inner emptiness, deprivation and worthlessness.

Loneliness is the surprising opportunity to know God.

Isaiah 41:10 . . . fear not, for I am with you; be not dismayed, for I am your God;

James 4:8 Draw near to God, and he will draw near to you.

Hebrews 13:5 Keep your life free from love of money, and be content with what you have, for he has said, "I will never leave you nor forsake you."

Notes:

June 18th

Love

There are four Greek words for love:

Philia – is the love expressed between friends

Storge – is the love seen in a family

Eros – an intense physical love, the kind of love shared between a man and a woman in marriage.

Agape – the kind of love found in the heart of the Deity – an unconditional love; the love that does not depend on any answering love in the heart of the one it loves.

C. S. Lewis.

John 15:13 The greatest love a person can have for his friends is to give his life for them. GNB.

John 3:16 For God so loved the world, that he gave his only Son, that whoever believes in him should not perish but have eternal life.

Notes:

Love

Love is basically a response – we love because we are loved.

One of life's greatest purposes is to receive God's love, and the channelling of that love into the lives of those around us who are weak and wounded.

John 15:12 "This is my (Jesus) commandment, that you love one another as I have loved you."

1 John 4:21 And this commandment we have from him: whoever loves God must also love his brother.

1 Cor. 8:3 But if anyone loves God, he is known by God.

Notes:

Love

Love means meeting needs.

Love is to have a reverence for Him, what pleases Him and to hate what He hates.

Love is to know Him, to learn His will and to please Him.

Divine love seeks our highest good.

---

1 John 4:7 Dear friends, let us love one another, because love comes from God. Whoever loves is a child of God and knows God. Whoever does not love does not know God, for God is love. GNB.

Romans 12:10 Love one another with brotherly affection.

1 John 5:3 For this is the love of God, that we keep his commandments.

Notes:

Love

God's love is an exercise of His goodness towards individual sinners whereby, having identified Himself with their welfare, He has given His son to be their Saviour, and now brings them to know and enjoy Him in a covenant relationship.

J. I. Packer

Ecclesiastes 5:10 He who loves money will not be satisfied with money, nor he who loves wealth with his income;

2 Thess. 3:5 May the Lord lead you into a greater understanding of God's love and the endurance that is given by Christ. GNB.

1 John 4:18 There is no fear in love; perfect love drives out all fear. GNB.

Notes:

June 22nd

Love

Love is an act of will. It is something we do, rather than feel. We have to work at it.

Don't worry about feeling love, just give what you would like to get. *Joy Davidman*

Love doesn't begin until there is no thought of return.

---

2 Cor. 5:14 We are ruled by the love of Christ, now that we recognize that one man died for everyone, which means that all share in his death. GNB.

1 John 4:12 No one has ever seen God; if we love one another, God abides in us and his love is perfected in us.

Notes:

Love

Love is to move towards another person without self-protection and to esteem others greater than ourselves.

Love is bringing about of the highest good in the life of another individual. *Charles Finney*

Love is giving, not getting.

---

1 Peter 4:8 Above everything, love one another earnestly, because love covers over many sins. GNB.

1 Thess. 4:9 Now concerning brotherly love you have no need for anyone to write to you, for you yourselves have been taught by God to love one another . . .

Notes:

June 24th

Love

If you take love out of an angel, what do you have left? – a devil.

If you take love out of a human being, what do you have left? – a sinner.

If you take love out of God, what do you have left? – nothing.

The first duty of love is to listen. *Paul Tillich*

Romans 8:28 And we know that for those who love God all things work together for good, for those who are called according to his purpose.

Proverbs 3:12 The LORD corrects those he loves, as parents correct a child of whom they are proud. GNB.

Notes:

Love

All Christians ought to love one another, but I don't necessarily think all Christians ought to work with one another.

Oswald Chambers

Real love is a decision. It is choosing to make an unconditional commitment to an imperfect person.

Matthew 5:44 But I (Jesus) say to you, Love your enemies and pray for those who persecute you, so that you may be sons of your Father who is in heaven.

Psalm 103:8 The LORD is merciful and gracious, slow to anger and abounding in steadfast love.

Notes:

June 26th

Love

You do not love the Lord at all, unless you love the souls of others. *C. H. Spurgeon*

Love is not just something you say, love is something you do.

Love seeks to know Him, to learn His will and please Him.

Matthew 10:37 Whoever loves father or mother more than me is not worthy of me, and whoever loves son or daughter more than me is not worthy of me.

1 John 3:1 See how much the Father has loved us! His love is so great that we are called God's children – and so, in fact, we are. GNB.

Notes:

Love

The more His love enters into us, the more fear will flow out of us.

How do you deepen and enrich your love for Christ? Focus your gaze on how much He loves you. We love because He first loved us. *Selwyn Hughes*

---

1 Chron. 16:34 Oh give thanks to the LORD, for he is good; for his steadfast love endures forever!

Hebrews 10:24 And let us consider how to stir up one another to love and good works . . .

1 John 2:10 Whoever loves his brother abides in the light . . .

Notes:

June 28th

Love

God's love is an action, not a reaction. His love depends not on what we are, but on what He is. He loves us because He is love.

Love cannot be love unless it has faithfulness in it.

---

1 John 4:9 And God showed his love for us by sending his only Son into the world, so that we might have life through him. GNB.

Romans 12:9 Let love be genuine. Abhor what is evil; hold fast to what is good.

Notes:

Love

Love is spontaneous, but it has to be maintained by discipline.
Oswald Chambers

Love can always wait to give: lust can never wait to get.

I really only love God as much as I love the person I love the least.
Dorothy Day

Psalm 36:5 Your steadfast love, O LORD, extends to the heavens, your faithfulness to the clouds.

1 John 3:11 For this is the message that you have heard from the beginning, that we should love one another.

Gal. 5:22 But the fruit of the Spirit is love . . .

Notes:

Love

God is love, which means that the energy that flows out from His Being is that of infinite eternal beneficence.

Love is investing my resources in someone else's well-being.

Self-love is healthy, love of self is unhealthy.

Romans 5:8 but God shows his love for us in that while we were still sinners, Christ died for us.

John 15:9 As the Father has loved me (Jesus), so have I loved you. Abide in my love.

Isaiah 61:8 For I the LORD love justice;

Notes:

Love

How much we love Him is far more important than how much we serve Him.

He loves each of us as if we are the only one there is to love.

Love, not nails, kept Christ on the cross.

John 14:21 Whoever has my commandments and keeps them, he it is who loves me. And he who loves me will be loved by my Father, and I will love him and manifest myself to him.

Hebrews 12:5,6 ". . . My child, pay attention when the Lord corrects you, and do not be discouraged when he rebukes you. Because the Lord corrects everyone he loves, and punishes everyone he accepts as his child." GNB.

Notes:

July 2nd

Love

It is not possible to draw any conclusion about God's love for us on the basis of the circumstances he brings into our life.

They do not love, who do not show their love.

Love is understanding and uncompromising.

John 14:15 "If you love me (Jesus), you will keep my commandments."

1 John 5:2 This is how we know that we love God's children: it is by loving God and obeying his commands. GNB.

Eph. 5:2 And walk in love, as Christ loved us and gave himself up for us, a fragrant offering and sacrifice to God.

Notes:

Love

God's love is uninfluenced, free, spontaneous, uncaused. It is eternal and Holy.

God desires to bring me to the place where I can trust His love, even though I cannot comprehend His purposes.

S.Hughes

Love is to accept the other person as they really are.

---

1 John 3:18 Little children, let us not love in word or talk but in deed and in truth.

Romans 13:8 Be under obligation to no one – the only obligation you have is to love one another. Whoever does this has obeyed the Law. GNB.

Amos 5:15 Hate evil, and love good . . .

Notes:

July 4th

Love

Love is not getting what I want, but giving to what my partner needs.

Love is not always an emotional experience, but rather a deliberate attempt to put the welfare and interests of others before our own.

Love is commitment.

Romans 13:10 If you love someone, you will never do them wrong; to love, then, is to obey the whole Law. GNB.

Eph. 5:25 Husbands, love your wives, as Christ loved the church and gave himself up for her . . .

1 John 2:15 Do not love the world or the things in the world.

Notes:

Love

Love is:

- listening.
- allowing each person to be themselves instead of pushing them into a mould.
- praying for the good of each church member.
- being tactful.
- seeking out the lonely.
- work.
- joyful service.
- not discussing the flaws of others.

---

1 Cor. 13:4-8 Love is patient and kind; love does not envy or boast; it is not arrogant or rude. It does not insist on its own way; it is not irritable or resentful; it does not rejoice at wrongdoing, but rejoices with the truth. Love bears all things, believes all things, hopes all things, endures all things. Love never ends.

Notes:

July 6th

Love

Love is:

- – something a person does.
- – agreeing whenever I can.
- – speaking words of encouragement.
- – being friendly.
- – sitting next to someone on a church bench, instead of alone when it's convenient.
- – remembering (joys, sorrows, family concerns and special days) and making mention of them to individuals.

---

1 John 4:10,11 This is what love is: it is not that we have loved God, but that he loved us and sent his Son to be the means by which our sins are forgiven. Dear friends, if this is how God loved us, then we should love one another. GNB.

Notes:

July 7th

Love

The people who need it the most, often desire it the least.

Though God loves us as we are, He loves us too much to let us stay as we are.

Love does not focus on rights, but on responsibility.

John 13:34,35 A new commandment I (Jesus) give to you, that you love one another: just as I have loved you, you also are to love one another. By this all people will know that you are my disciples, if you have love for one another.

Notes:

July 8th

Love

Attend to the cross! Sit before it, meditate upon it. Heaven knows no higher strategy for begetting love in human hearts than to bring a person to the cross, hold him there, until they see in that bleeding sagging figure on the tree, just how much God loves them. *Dr. W. E. Sangster*

---

1 John 4:16 . . . God is love, and those who live in love live in union with God and God lives in union with them. GNB.

Deut. 6:5 You shall love the LORD your God with all your heart and with all your soul and with all your might.

Notes:

Maturity

Spiritual maturity is the ability to respond to life and to any given situation in the same way that Jesus would. It is not a matter of age, but of attitude. It is not a destination, but a direction. It is moving through life with godly intent and purpose.

Selwyn Hughes

1 Cor. 14:20 Brothers, do not be children in your thinking. Be infants in evil, but in your thinking be mature.

2 Thess. 1:3 We ought always to give thanks to God for you, brothers, as is right, because your faith is growing abundantly, and the love of every one of you for one another is increasing.

Notes:

Maturity

Christian maturity is maturity by gazing – at Jesus.

The proof of spiritual maturity is not how "pure" you are, but being aware of your impurity. *Philip Yancey*

Christian maturity can be slow and painful.

Our Christian maturity can be measured by asking ourselves, "Where do I put my dependency?"

---

2 Cor. 7:1 Since we have these promises, beloved, let us cleanse ourselves from every defilement of body and spirit, bringing holiness to completion in the fear of God.

Luke 2:52 And Jesus increased in wisdom and in stature and in favour with God and man.

Notes:

Maturity

Maturity is the process by which we are changed from an unnatural coil around the wrong centre to a natural coil around God as the centre.

To stand still in the Christian life is to go back. To go forwards means to go back to the cross.

Romans 12:2 Do not be conformed to this world, but be transformed by the renewal of your mind, that by testing you may discern what is the will of God, what is good and acceptable and perfect.

Hebrews 5:14 But solid food is for the mature, for those who have their powers of discernment trained by constant practice to distinguish good from evil.

Notes:

July 12th

Maturity

Maturity is the ability to live in someone else's world and not complain.

Maturity is not arriving, but proceeding in the right direction.

There is no strain in maturity, it is relaxed.

The central thing in maturity is fellowship.

E. Stanley Jones

1 Cor. 13:11 When I (Paul) was a child, I spoke like a child, I thought like a child, I reasoned like a child. When I became a man, I gave up childish ways.

Hebrews 6:1 Let us go forward, then, to mature teaching and leave behind us the first lessons of the Christian message. GNB.

Notes:

Maturity

Maturity is a quiet and steady change.

Marks of maturity:

1. The willingness to accept the responsibility of being what you are.
2. Dependent trust.
3. An obedient heart.
4. A willingness to face and feel everything that goes on inside us.
5. Deep perennial joy.
6. An ability to relate to others.

(Continued tomorrow)

Col. 1:28 Him (Jesus) we proclaim, warning everyone and teaching everyone with all wisdom, that we may present everyone mature in Christ.

Phil. 1:6 And I am sure of this, that he who began a good work in you will bring it to completion at the day of Jesus Christ.

Notes:

July 14th

Maturity

(Continued from yesterday)

7. Having an "other-centred" concern and being more controlled by love for people than a fear of being hurt.
8. Projecting yourself into the position of others and seeing things from their point of view.
9. A strong sense of morality.
10. A continuing thirst after God.
11. An out flowing love.

Maturity in the Christian life is not measured by what a man knows, but by what he does.

J. Dwight Pentecost

Phil. 3:14,15 So I (Paul) run straight towards the goal in order to win the prize, which is God's call through Christ Jesus to the life above. All of us who are spiritually mature should have this same attitude. GNB.

2 Peter 3:18 But grow in the grace and knowledge of our Lord and Saviour Jesus Christ.

Notes:

Meditation

Meditation is the process of holding a verse of Scripture in the mind, pondering it, continually contemplating it, dwelling upon it, viewing it from every angle of imagination until it begins to affect the deepest part of one's spiritual being.

Selwyn Hughes

Psalm 77:12 I will ponder all your work, and meditate on your mighty deeds.

Psalm 119:97 Oh how I love your law! It is my meditation all the day.

Psalm 104:34 May my meditation be pleasing to him, for I rejoice in the LORD.

Notes:

Meditation

Meditation is commencing with one's own heart – taking a Biblical truth or thought, reflecting on it, pondering it and mulling it over, until the spiritual wisdom contained in it passes from the mind into the heart.

Meditation is rolling things around in your mind.

Psalm 119:99 I understand more than all my teachers, because I meditate on your instructions. GNB.

Psalm 19:14 Let the words of my mouth and the meditation of my heart be acceptable in your sight, O LORD, my rock and my redeemer.

Notes:

Meditation

Meditation is thinking about Scripture with a view to understanding it and doing what it says.

Meditation is simply thought prolonged and directed to a single object.
A. T. Pierson

Meditation is holding the word of God in your heart and mind until it has affected every area of your life.
Andrew Murray

Psalm 1:2 but his delight is in the law of the LORD, and on his law he meditates day and night.

Psalm 63:5,6 My soul will be satisfied . . . and my mouth will praise you . . . when I remember you upon my bed, and meditate on you in the watches of the night;

Notes:

July 18th

Meditation

Meditation is equivalent to rumination. Just as a ruminant animal gets its nutrition and energy from what it eats through regurgitation, so a Christian extracts from the Scripture the life of God through meditation.

Selwyn Hughes

Meditation is deep, focused thinking.

Psalm 119:48 I respect and love your commandments; I will meditate on your instructions. GNB.

Psalm 143:5 I remember the days of old; I meditate on all that you have done; I ponder the work of your hands.

Notes:

Meekness

The meek person in the Biblical sense is not timid, shy, hesitant and unassuming, but trusting, confident and secure.

Meekness is a passive trait, describing the proper Christian response when others mistreat us.

Meekness is controlled strength.

Meekness is accepting God's chastisement.

James 1:21 Therefore put away all filthiness and rampant wickedness and receive with meekness the implanted word, which is able to save your souls.

Isaiah 29:19 The meek shall obtain fresh joy in the LORD . . .

Matthew 5:5 Blessed are the meek, for they shall inherit the earth.

Notes:

July 20th

Mercy

God in His mercy does not give us what we do deserve, and God in His grace gives us what we do not deserve.

Mercy is a sense of pity plus a desire to relieve the suffering, i.e. pity plus action. *D. M. Lloyd-Jones*

Psalm 103:8 The LORD is merciful and gracious, slow to anger and abounding in steadfast love.

Matthew 5:7 Blessed are the merciful, for they shall receive mercy.

Deut. 4:31 For the LORD your God is a merciful God.

Notes:

Mercy

Mercy is a melting disposition whereby we lay to heart miseries of others and are ready on all occasions to be instrumental for their good. *Thomas Watson*

We need mercy to help cleanse us from sin.

Mercy is compassion plus action.

Psalm 23:6 Surely goodness and mercy shall follow me all the days of my life . . .

Eph. 2:4 But God's mercy is so abundant, and his love for us is so great, that while we were spiritually dead in our disobedience he brought us to life with Christ. GNB.

Matthew 9:13 . . . I (Jesus) desire mercy, and not sacrifice.

Notes:

Money

The true Christian ought to be more afraid of being rich, than of being poor. *J. C. Ryle*

We cannot serve God and mammon, but we can serve God with mammon.

Prosperity is more perilous to the soul, than adversity to the body. St. Augustine

---

Proverbs 3:9 Honour the LORD with your wealth and with the firstfruits of all your produce;

1 Tim. 6:10 For the love of money is a root of all kinds of evils.

Proverbs 11:28 Whoever trusts in his riches will fall, but the righteous will flourish like a green leaf.

Notes:

Money

Money increases your appetite, but not your satisfaction.

Derek Tidball

The love of money can get our priorities out of line. We must keep reminding ourselves that God must be first in our lives and that money cannot satisfy our deepest needs.

Ecclesiastes 5:10 He who loves money will not be satisfied with money, nor he who loves wealth with his income;

1 John 3:17 Rich people who see a brother or sister in need, yet close their hearts against them, cannot claim that they love God. GNB.

Notes:

July 24th

Money

Money is a universal passport for everything but happiness, and a passport everywhere but to Heaven.

Selwyn Hughes

Money is like seawater, the more you drink, the more you want.

God doesn't want our money or certain things – He wants us.

Acts 8:20 But Peter said to him (Simon), "May your silver perish with you, because you thought you could obtain the gift of God with money!"

Hebrews 13:5 Keep your life free from love of money . . .

Matthew 6:24 You cannot serve God and money.

Notes:

Obedience

Obedience is doing what we are told to do, when we are told to do it, with the right heart attitude.

Only he who believes is obedient, only he who is obedient believes. *Dietrich Bonhoeffer*

Obedience is the door that lets Christ in.

God blesses obedience.

Exodus 19:5,6 Now therefore, if you will indeed obey my voice and keep my covenant, you shall be my treasured possession among all peoples . . . and you shall be to me a kingdom of priests and a holy nation.

Notes:

July 26th

Obedience

Obedience is the greatest issue in the Christian life.

The golden rule for understanding spirituality is not intellect, but obedience. *Oswald Chambers*

The Bible is insistent that isolated external acts of homage to God cannot make up for a lack of consistent obedience in heart and conduct.

---

1 Samuel 15:22 And Samuel said, "Has the LORD as great delight in burnt offerings and sacrifices, as in obeying the voice of the LORD? Behold, to obey is better than sacrifice . . ."

Acts 5:29 But Peter and the apostles answered, "We must obey God rather than men."

Notes:

Obedience

Obedience is the only place of safety for Christians.

Selwyn Hughes

Don't spoil tomorrow by failing to obey God today.

Light obeyed increases light. Light rejected bringeth night.

God will never reveal more truth about Himself until you have obeyed what you already know. *Oswald Chambers*

Romans 6:17 But thanks be to God! For though at one time you were slaves to sin, you have obeyed with all your heart the truths found in the teaching you received. GNB.

Hebrews 5:8 Although he (Jesus) was a son, he learned obedience through what he suffered.

Notes:

July 28th

Obedience

No one can hope to know God unless they are prepared to obey Him.

All God's revelations are sealed until they are opened to us by obedience. *Oswald Chambers*

God demands obedience, but our obedience is not to be governed by our convenience.

Titus 3:1 Remind your people to submit to rulers and authorities, to obey them, and to be ready to do good in every way. GNB.

Phil. 2:8 And being found in human form, he (Jesus) humbled himself by becoming obedient to the point of death, even death on a cross.

Notes:

Obedience

Obedience is not legalism, but the outworking of love.

Are we obeying that thing that God has got His finger on in our lives? Nothing can substitute for obedience.

The place where you lose God's presence is always at the point of disobedience.

Jeremiah 7:23,24 But this command I gave them (your fathers): 'Obey my voice, and I will be your God, and you shall be my people. And walk in all the way that I command you, that it may be well with you.' But they did not obey or incline their ear, but walked in their own counsels and the stubbornness of their evil hearts, and went backwards and not forwards.

Notes:

July 30th

Obedience

The secret of obeying is loving.

Each act of obedience by the Christian is a modest proof, unequivocal for all its imperfection, of the reality of what he attests. *Karl Barth*

To know God is to obey Him, and to obey Him is to know Him.

Deut. 13:4 You shall walk after the LORD your God and fear him and keep his commandments and obey his voice, and you shall serve him and hold fast to him.

Romans 5:19 For as by the one man's disobedience the many were made sinners, so by the one man's obedience the many will be made righteous.

Joshua 24:24 And the people said to Joshua, "The LORD our God we will serve, and his voice we will obey."

Notes:

Peace

Am I a peacemaker or a piece-maker?

If we would make peace with the world, the world would leave us alone. *John Newton*

Peace is joy with its arms folded in deep assurance.

Peace is not absence of danger, but the presence of God.

John 16:33 I (Jesus) have said these things to you, that in me you may have peace.

Romans 14:19 So then, we must always aim at those things that bring peace and that help to strengthen one another. GNB.

2 Thess. 3:16 Now may the Lord of peace himself give you peace at all times in every way.

Notes:

August 1st

Peace

Peace is the comfortable sense of our reconciliation to God, an interest in His favour, and the hope of the heavenly blessedness and enjoyment of God hereafter.

Whenever you obey God, His seal is always that of peace.

Oswald Chambers

Col. 3:15 And let the peace of Christ rule in your hearts . . .

Romans 8:6 To set the mind on the flesh is death, but to set the mind on the Spirit is life and peace.

Gal. 5:22 But the fruit of the Spirit is . . . peace.

Hebrews 12:14 Strive for peace with everyone . . .

Notes:

Peace

Peace can only be found in full commitment.

The believer must continually ask, "will I have peace within if I do this or do that?" *Hendriksen*

No soul can experience deep inner peace unless it rests ultimately in the goodness of God. *Selwyn Hughes*

---

1 Cor. 14:33 For God is not a God of confusion but of peace.

Phil. 4:7 And God's peace, which is far beyond human understanding, will keep your hearts and minds safe in union with Christ Jesus. GNB.

Eph. 2:14 For he (Jesus) himself is our peace . . .

Notes:

August 3rd

Praise

Praise means to speak well of, to exalt, to honour.

We thank God for what He does – we praise Him for who He is.

We can only really give God two things; our praise and our prayer.

Hebrews 13:15 Let us, then, always offer praise to God as our sacrifice through Jesus, which is the offering presented by lips that confess him as Lord. GNB.

Psalm 34:1 I will bless the LORD at all times; his praise shall continually be in my mouth.

Notes:

Praise

Praise is the outflow of a heart which finds satisfaction in God.

Praise is the highest activity of the redeemed man or woman.

Praise is the soil in which joy thrives.

Praise is a choice.

Psalm 92:1 It is good to give thanks to the LORD, to sing praises to your name, O Most High;

Luke 2:20 The shepherds went back, singing praises to God for all they had heard and seen; GNB.

Psalm 139:14 I praise you, for I am fearfully and wonderfully made.

Notes:

August 5th

Prayer

Never make any plans unless you are willing to have God change them and never pray unless you are willing to accept God's answer.

All needs are met on our knees.

Prayer is taking part in the process of being deeply known.

C. S. Lewis

Matthew 6: 9,10 Pray then like this:

"Our Father in heaven,
hallowed be your name.
Your kingdom come,
your will be done,
on earth as it is in heaven.

Notes:

Prayer

The most important measure of prayer is not its length, but its depth; not its beautiful words, but its intensity.

The prayer house is the powerhouse. *C. H. Spurgeon*

Prayer moves the hand that moves the world.

More things are wrought in Heaven and earth through prayer than this world dreams of.

Matthew 6:11,12,13

Give us this day our daily bread,
and forgive us our debts,
as we also have forgiven our debtors.
And lead us not into temptation,
but deliver us from evil."

Notes:

August 7th

Prayer

The conditions of prayer:

1. Pray in the name of God's son, Jesus.
2. For God's glory and not for selfish reasons.
3. According to God's will, not our own.
4. Believe, praying in faith.

The first rule of prayer is honesty. *Martin Luther*

Backsliding begins when knee-bending stops.

---

2 Chron. 7:14 . . . if my people who are called by my name humble themselves, and pray and seek my face and turn from their wicked ways, then I will hear from heaven and will forgive their sin and heal their land.

Matthew 21:22 And whatever you ask in prayer, you will receive, if you have faith.

Notes:

Prayer

Nothing lies beyond the reach of prayer, except that which is outside the will of God.

True prayer – the prayer that must be answered – is the personal recognition and acceptance of the divine will.

Westcott

We must abide in the Lord, not allowing sin in our lives, and pray with thanksgiving.

Luke 18:1 And he (Jesus) told them a parable to the effect that they ought always to pray and not lose heart.

John 17:9 I (Jesus) am praying for them. I am not praying for the world but for those whom you (Father) have given me, for they are yours.

Notes:

August 9th

Prayer

Our prayers are God talking to himself. *C. S. Lewis*

The primary purpose of prayer is to bring the whole of life into the presence of God for cleansing and decision making.

Prayer is designed for man – not man for prayer.

When I stop praying, the coincidences stop happening.
William Temple

Rev. 5:8 And when he (the Lamb) had taken the scroll, the four living creatures and the twenty-four elders fell down before the Lamb, each holding a harp, and golden bowls full of incense, which are the prayers of the saints.

Matthew 26:41 Watch and pray that you may not enter into temptation. The spirit indeed is willing, but the flesh is weak.

Notes:

Prayer

Seven prayerless days make one weak.

The idea of prayer is not in order to get answers from God; prayer is perfect and complete oneness with God. The Biblical idea of prayer is that we may get to know God Himself. *Oswald Chambers*

Prayer is co-operation with God.

Mark 1:35 And rising very early in the morning, while it was still dark, he (Jesus) departed and went out to a desolate place, and there he prayed.

Romans 12:12 Rejoice in hope, be patient in tribulation, be constant in prayer.

Notes:

Prayer

Prayerlessness is sin, because it despises the sacrifice made on the cross by Christ, it encourages us to depend on our own resources and deprives the Christian Church of power.

Prayer is a dialogue not a monologue.

Life's best outlook is a prayerful uplook.

Acts 4:31 And when they had prayed, the place in which they were gathered together was shaken, and they were all filled with the Holy Spirit and continued to speak the word of God with boldness.

1 Samuel 12:23 Moreover, as for me (Samuel), far be it from me that I should sin against the LORD by ceasing to pray for you . . .

Notes:

Prayer

It is not the body's posture when we pray but the heart's attitude that counts. *Billy Graham*

The key prayer is that we may love what God commands and desire what He promises. *R. V. G. Tasker*

We can lose our intimacy with God by prayerlessness and carelessness.

---

1 John 5:14 And this is the confidence that we have towards him, that if we ask anything according to his will he hears us.

Eph. 1:16 . . . I (Paul) do not cease to give thanks for you, remembering you in my prayers . . .

Col. 4:2 Be persistent in prayer, and keep alert as you pray, giving thanks to God. GNB.

Notes:

August 13th

Prayer

Prayer is telling God, day-by-day, in what ways we feel that we are helpless. My helplessness is Jesus knocking at my heart's door.

When it is hardest to pray, we ought to pray harder.

D. L. Moody

Why pray when you can worry!

Nehemiah 1:11 O Lord, let your ear be attentive to the prayer of your servant, and to the prayer of your servants who delight to fear your name . . .

Romans 8:26 In the same way the Spirit also comes to help us, weak as we are. For we do not know how we ought to pray; the Spirit himself pleads with God for us in groans that words cannot express. GNB.

Notes:

Prayer

Praying:

1. We never become backsliders on our knees.
2. He who kneels lowest, rises highest.
3. He stands strongest, who kneels longest.

Prayer is problematic because it is not automatic, but "right, earnest work". *Jacob Boehme*

The best way to look for God is sometimes on your knees.

Rev. 8:3,4 And another angel came and stood at the altar with a golden censer, and he was given much incense to offer with the prayers of all the saints on the golden altar before the throne, and the smoke of the incense, with the prayers of the saints, rose before God from the hand of the angel.

Notes:

August 15th

Prayer

Prayer is not primarily God's way of getting things done, but giving the Church 'on the job' training in overcoming the forces hostile to God.

Prayer is given and ordained for the purpose of glorifying God. *O. Hallesby*

Prayer is not prattle, but a battle.

Luke 6:12 At that time Jesus went up a hill to pray and spent the whole night there praying to God. GNB.

Acts 2:42 And they (the believers) devoted themselves to the apostles teaching and fellowship, to the breaking of bread and the prayers.

Notes:

Prayer

Prayer is the debating chamber of the soul – an area of argument where God has the chance to win the debate.

Prayer is more than a demand, it is also a desire.

Prayer is digging up the treasures that God has already prepared for us. *John Calvin*

Phil. 4:6,7 . . . do not be anxious about anything, but in everything by prayer and supplication with thanksgiving let your requests be made known to God. And the peace of God, which surpasses all understanding, will guard your hearts and your minds in Christ Jesus.

Luke 5:16 But he (Jesus) would go away to lonely places, where he prayed. GNB.

Notes:

August 17th

Prayer

Prayer is our response to the God who speaks to us.

Prayer may not remove the affliction, but it can transform it.

R. V. G. Tasker

You can do lots of things once you have prayed, but you can do nothing until you have prayed.

Prayer is relaxed receptivity.

---

1 Peter 3:12 For the eyes of the Lord are on the righteous, and his ears are open to their prayer.

Luke 22:31,32 "Simon, Simon, behold, Satan demanded to have you, that he might sift you like wheat, but I (Jesus) have prayed for you that your faith may not fail."

Notes:

Prayer

'Forward on our knees' should be the watch cry of all believers.

If it's big enough to worry about, it's big enough to pray about.

Everything we do in the Christian life is easier than prayer.

Dr. M. Lloyd-Jones

We should pray for wings not crutches.

Col. 1:9 For this reason we have always prayed for you, ever since we heard about you. We ask God to fill you with the knowledge of his will, with all the wisdom and understanding that his Spirit gives. GNB.

1 Thess. 5:17 . . . pray without ceasing . . .

Notes:

August 19th

Prayer

We must prepare as if everything depends on us and pray as if everything depends on God.

I never get time to pray – I've always got to make it.

Dr. Wilber Smith

Prayer and helplessness are inseparable. Only he who is helpless can truly pray. *O. Hallesby*

James 5:16 Therefore, confess your sins to one another and pray for one another, that you may be healed. The prayer of a righteous person has great power as it is working.

Luke 22:44 And being in an agony he (Jesus) prayed more earnestly;

Notes:

Prayer

We shall with God's help seek to work for what we pray for and pray for what we work for.

God does nothing redemptively except by prayer.

John Wesley

Prayer doesn't necessarily change things for you, but it changes you for things.

Luke 9:18 One day when Jesus was praying alone, the disciples came to him. GNB.

1 Samuel 1:27 For this child I (Hannah) prayed, and the LORD has granted me my petition that I made to him.

Matthew 5:44,45 But I (Jesus) say to you, Love your enemies and pray for those who persecute you, so that you may be sons of your Father who is in heaven.

Notes:

August 21st

Prayer

Prayer is not overcoming God's reluctance, but laying hold on His highest willingness.

Prayer is the key of the morning and the lock of the night.

C. H. Spurgeon

We lie to God in prayer if we do not rely upon Him after prayer.

Matthew 9:37,38 So he (Jesus) said to his disciples, "The harvest is large, but there are few workers to gather it in. Pray to the owner of the harvest that he will send out workers to gather in his harvest." GNB.

Acts 1:14 All these with one accord were devoting themselves to prayer . . .

Notes:

Prayer

I often say my prayers,
But do I ever pray,
And do the wishes of my heart,
Go with the words I say?

We pray for silver, but God often gives us gold instead.

Martin Luther

God does not just answer prayer, He answers you.

---

1 Tim. 2:1 First of all, then, I urge that supplications, prayers, intercessions, and thanksgivings be made for all people . . .

Proverbs 15:29 When good people pray, the LORD listens, but he ignores those who are evil. GNB.

Notes:

Prayer

Prayer is a difficult habit to acquire – an easy one to lose.

God wants us to pray, not because He likes to hear the sound of our voice, but because He wants to answer our prayer.

God's delays to prayer are not necessarily denials.

No prayer, no power.

Mark 14:38 And he (Jesus) said to them, "Keep watch, and pray that you will not fall into temptation. The spirit is willing, but the flesh is weak." GNB.

Jude 20 But you, beloved, build yourselves up in your most holy faith; pray in the Holy Spirit;

Notes:

Prayer

Prayer is aligning ourselves with the purposes of God.

Someone has said there are two ways of handling life's problems; we can either let them drive us to despair, or drive us to prayer.

God's help is but a prayer away.

Matthew 6:6 But when you pray, go into your room and shut the door and pray to your Father who is in secret. And your Father who sees in secret will reward you.

Mark 6:46 And after he (Jesus) had taken leave of them (the disciples), he went up on the mountain to pray.

Notes:

August 25th

Prayer

Prayer is a way to get what God wants, not what I want.

God always answers prayers by saying yes, no, or not just now as I will give you something better.

Prayer is the will to cooperate with God in the whole of one's life.

Luke 22:41,42 And he (Jesus) withdrew from them about a stone's throw, and knelt down and prayed, saying, "Father, if you are willing, remove this cup from me. Nevertheless, not my will, but yours, be done."

John 14:13 Whatever you ask in my name, this I (Jesus) will do, that the Father may be glorified in the Son.

Notes:

Prayer

Prayer trusts as if the whole thing depends on God, and works as if the whole thing depends on us.

We kneel, how weak – we rise, how full of power.

If you don't make time to pray, you end up not having any time to pray.

Mark 11:25 And whenever you stand praying, forgive, if you have anything against anyone, so that your Father also who is in heaven may forgive you your trespasses.

Eph. 6:18 . . . praying at all times in the Spirit, with all prayer and supplication.

James 5:13 Is anyone among you suffering? Let him pray.

Notes:

August 27th

Prayer

Prayer does not fit us for greater works; prayer is the greater works. *Oswald Chambers*

We can do so much more than pray, after we have prayed, but we cannot do more than pray until we have prayed.

Prayer is an effort of the will.

Mark 11:24 Therefore I tell you, whatever you ask in prayer, believe that you have received it, and it will be yours.

Psalm 91:15 When they call to me, I will answer them; when they are in trouble, I will be with them. GNB.

Notes:

Pride

Pride is the primal sin and the foulest of them all. It causes one to put oneself in the centre of life, which is God's place.

Pride is the ego in the place God wants to be.

Pride is the deification of self. *Oswald Chambers*

Proverbs 29:23 One's pride will bring him low, but he who is lowly in spirit will obtain honour.

1 John 2:16 For all that is in the world – the desires of the flesh and the desires of the eyes and pride in possessions – is not from the Father but is from the world.

Notes:

August 29th

Pride

Pride gives self, not God, the supreme position.

Pride robs God of his rightful place at the centre of our lives.

That which first overcame man is the last thing he overcomes. *St. Augustine*

Pride is simply independence from God.

Psalm 10:4 The wicked do not care about the LORD; in their pride they think that God doesn't matter. GNB.

Proverbs 16:18 Pride goes before destruction, and a haughty spirit before a fall.

Proverbs 11:2 When pride comes, then comes disgrace, but with the humble is wisdom.

Notes:

Pride

Pride is believing that I achieved what in reality God and others did for me and through me. *Selwyn Hughes*

In respect of pride, some Christians grow; others just swell!

Pride must die in you, or Christ cannot live in you.
William Law

Proverbs 8:13 Pride and arrogance and the way of evil and perverted speech I hate.

Mark 7:21,22,23 For from the inside, from a person's heart, come the evil ideas which lead him to do immoral things . . . and do all sorts of evil things; deceit, indecency, jealousy, slander, pride, and folly - all these evil things come from inside a person and make him unclean. GNB.

Notes:

August 31st

Prophecy

A prophet brings the Word of God and applies it to specific situations.

The word "prophecy" has within it two elements – forthtelling and foretelling. *Selwyn Hughes*

Seven tests for prophecy:

1. Does it glorify God?
2. Is it in accord with scriptures?

(Continued tomorrow)

Joel 2:28 "And it shall come to pass afterwards, that I will pour out my Spirit on all flesh; your sons and your daughters shall prophesy . . ."

1 Cor. 14:5 Now I want you all to speak in tongues, but even more to prophesy.

Notes:

Prophecy

(Continued from yesterday)

3. Does the supposed prophecy build up the Church?
4. Is it spoken with love?
5. Does the speaker submit to the judgement and consensus of others?
6. Is the speaker in control of himself?
7. Is there too much of it?

Romans 12:6 Having gifts that differ according to the grace given to us, let us use them: if prophecy, in proportion to our faith;

1 Cor. 14:29 Let two or three prophets speak, and let the others weigh what is said.

Notes:

September 2nd

Propitiation

Propitiation means averting God's anger with an offering.

Propitiation is a sacrifice that averts wrath through expiating sin and cancelling guilt. *J. I. Packer*

Propitiation is God turning aside from us (who deserve it) His holy wrath and anger against sin and pouring it out instead upon His spotless Son (who deserves none of it).

---

1 John 2:2 He (Jesus) is the propitiation for our sins, and not for ours only but also for the sins of the whole world.

1 John 4:10 In this is love, not that we have loved God but that he loved us and sent his Son to be the propitiation for our sins.

Notes:

Redemption

Redemption is to achieve the transfer of ownership from one to another through the payment of a price or an equivalent substitute.

It is essentially the payment of a ransom for the release of a captive.

Col. 1:13,14 He (Jesus) has delivered us from the domain of darkness and transferred us to the kingdom of his beloved Son, in whom we have redemption, the forgiveness of sins.

Luke 1:68 "Blessed be the Lord God of Israel, for he has visited and redeemed his people . . ."

Notes:

September 4th

Redemption

Redemption is making us fit for fellowship with God.

Redemption is freeing from bondage and slavery by a work of mighty power – biblically this usually includes the payment of a price or ransom.

Redemption means I am now free from the debt of sin.

Romans 3:23,24 . . . for all have sinned and fall short of the glory of God, and are justified by his grace as a gift, through the redemption that is in Christ Jesus . . .

Eph. 1:7 In him (Jesus) we have redemption through his blood . . .

Notes:

Repentance

Repentance is a change of mind, leading to a change in direction. It is an action of the will by which we turn our back on all known sin.

Repentance is being sorry enough to stop sinning.

Repentance is a willing and glad change of heart and mind.

Romans 2:4 Surely you know that God is kind, because he is trying to lead you to repent. GNB.

Acts 3:19 Repent therefore, and turn again, that your sins may be blotted out . . .

Notes:

September 6th

Repentance

Repentance is taking sides with God against ourselves.

Repentance always brings a man to this point: I have sinned. *Oswald Chambers*

Repentance is not merely abandonment of sin, but a positive dependence on (or faith in) the Lord.

Repentance is a movement of the soul that is full speed astern. *C. S. Lewis*

Acts 26:20 First in Damascus and in Jerusalem and then in all Judea and among the Gentiles, I (Paul) preached that they must repent of their sins and turn to God and do the things that would show they had repented. GNB.

2 Cor. 7:10 For godly grief produces a repentance that leads to salvation without regret, whereas worldly grief produces death.

Notes:

Repentance

If we have truly repented it is not a one-time act. It is a lifelong business.

Giving up all controversy with God and admitting He is totally right on every point and that the sinner is totally wrong.
Charles Finney

Repentance is a turning of one's back on sin.

---

2 Peter 3:9 The Lord is not slow to fulfil his promise as some count slowness, but is patient towards you, not wishing that any should perish, but that all should reach repentance.

Matthew 3:8 Do those things that will show that you have turned from your sins. GNB.

Notes:

September 8th

Repentance

Repentance is binding one's conscience to God's moral law, confessing and forsaking one's sins, making restitution for past wrongs, grieving before God at the dishonour one's sins have done Him and forming a game plan for holy living.

J. I. Packer

Matthew 3:1,2 In those days John the Baptist came preaching in the wilderness of Judea, "Repent, for the kingdom of heaven is at hand."

Acts 17:30 The times of ignorance God overlooked, but now he commands all people everywhere to repent . . .

Notes:

Repentance

Repentance is the forerunner of deliverance.

Repentance is telling God one is sorry for having displaced Him from one's life, and that now He is to be allowed into one's life to rule and reign as one's rightful Lord.

The bedrock of Christianity is repentance.

Oswald Chambers

Ezekiel 14:6 . . . Thus says the Lord GOD: Repent and turn away from your idols, and turn away your faces from all your abominations.

Luke 5:32 I (Jesus) have not come to call the righteous but sinners to repentance.

Luke 24:46,47 . . . Thus it is written, that the Christ should suffer and on the third day rise from the dead, and that repentance and forgiveness of sins should be proclaimed in his name to all nations . . .

Notes:

September 10th

Repentance

To repent is to experience a shift in our perceived source of life.

Repentance is an about-face movement from denial and rebellion to truth and surrender – from death to life.

Repentance always involves an admission of wrongdoing – without excuse. *Selwyn Hughes*

Repentance is a turning from . . . to God.

Rev. 3:19 Those whom I love, I reprove and discipline, so be zealous and repent.

Job 42:6 . . . therefore I (Job) despise myself, and repent in dust and ashes.

Psalm 7:12 If a man does not repent, God will whet his sword;

Notes:

Repentance

Repentance is a change of mind about where life is found.

To repent means to rethink one's position, to realise one's foolishness and return to God with a sorrowful heart and a contrite spirit.

Repentance is agreeing with God.

Hebrews 6:4 For how can those who abandon their faith be brought back to repent again? GNB.

Rev. 2:5 Remember therefore from where you have fallen; repent, and do the works you did at first.

Notes:

September 12th

Repentance

Repentance is a change of mind that leads to a change of conduct.

Repentance infers that if we had the opportunity to commit sin again, we would not.

Repentance enables God to move into our lives with might and power. *Selwyn Hughes*

Repentance is always associated with judgement and mercy.

Mark 1:15 (Jesus said,) "The time is fulfilled, and the kingdom of God is at hand; repent and believe in the gospel."

Luke 17:3 "If your brother sins, rebuke him, and if he repents, forgive him . . ." GNB.

Notes:

Repentance

Repentance is a fundamental change of mind (honestly acknowledging personal guilt) of heart (sorrow for that sin) and of will (a desire and determination to forsake sin).

Repentance is a grace as well as a duty.

Repentance is a gift of God – the gift of tears.

Acts 2:38 And Peter said to them, "Repent and be baptised every one of you in the name of Jesus Christ for the forgiveness of your sins, and you will receive the gift of the Holy Spirit."

Luke 15:10 Just so, I (Jesus) tell you, there is joy before the angels of God over one sinner who repents.

Notes:

September 14th

Revival

Revival is heaven overflowing its banks producing in the Church such a sense of divine majesty and power that it causes Christians and non-Christians to stand in awe of the living God. *Selwyn Hughes*

Revival is a people saturated with God.

Zechariah 1:3 . . . Thus declares the Lord of hosts: Return to me, says the Lord of hosts, and I will return to you . . .

Romans 12:2 Do not conform yourselves to the standards of this world, but let God transform you inwardly by a complete change of your mind. GNB.

Notes:

Revival

Revival is God revealing Himself in awful holiness and irresistible power. It is such a manifest working of God that human personalities are overshadowed and human programmes abandoned. *A. Wallis*

Revival takes place when we experience "times of refreshing from the presence of the Lord."

Dr. J. Edwin Orr

Jeremiah 24:7 I will give them a heart to know that I am the LORD, and they shall be my people and I will be their God, for they shall return to me with their whole heart.

Notes:

September 16th

Revival

Three characteristics of revival:

1. An intense, palpable and extraordinary sense of God's presence.
2. A deep desire to be rid of all sin.
3. A powerful impact on the wider community.

Selwyn Hughes

Revival is not the top blowing off, but the bottom falling out. *Joe Church*

Deut. 4:29 But from there (the nations) you will seek the LORD your God and you will find him, if you search after him with all your heart and with all your soul.

Hosea 14:7 They (Israel) shall return and dwell beneath my shadow;

Notes:

Revival

True spiritual revival is an inrush of divine life into a body threatening to become a corpse. *D. M. Panton*

Revival is not a movement of men towards God so much as a movement of God amongst men.

Revival is an extraordinary work of a sovereign God that revitalises the Church and transforms society. *Pete Greig*

Hosea 10:12 It is time for you to turn to me, your LORD, and I will come and pour out blessings upon you. GNB.

Lam. 3:40 Let us test and examine our ways, and return to the LORD!

Notes:

September 18th

Revival

Four essential ingredients which need to be fulfilled before revival can come:

1. All sin must be confessed to God.
2. There must be no cloud between the believer and God and the believer and everyone else.
3. The Holy Spirit must not only be invited but obeyed.
4. There must be continued public confession of Christ as Saviour and Lord.

Evan Roberts

Ezekiel 11:19,20 And I (the LORD) will give them one heart, and a new spirit I will put within them. I will remove the heart of stone from their flesh and give them a heart of flesh, that they may walk in my statutes and keep my rules and obey them.

Psalm 19:7 The law of the LORD is perfect, reviving the soul;

Notes:

Revival

Revival is the sudden awesome and overwhelming flood of God's power upon a community of His people.

Selwyn Hughes

Revival does not bring saints to perfection in a day, but wakes up the drowsy.

True revival is not worked up; it is sent down.

Joel 2:12,13 "Yet even now", declares the LORD, "return to me with all your heart, with fasting, with weeping, and with mourning; and rend your hearts and not your garments." Return to the LORD, your God . . .

Ezekiel 36:26 I (the LORD) will give you a new heart and a new mind. I will take away your stubborn heart of stone and give you an obedient heart. GNB.

Notes:

September 20th

Revival

Revival comes when God's people earnestly want it and are willing to pay the price.

Revival is God bending down to the dying embers of a fire just about to go out and breathing into it until it bursts into flame. *Christmas Evans*

Isaiah 2:3 . . . and many peoples shall come, and say: "Come, let us go up to the mountain of the LORD, to the house of the God of Jacob, that he may teach us his ways and that we may walk in his paths."

Psalm 51:10 Create in me a clean heart, O God, and renew a right spirit within me.

Notes:

Revival

Revival is a movement of the Holy Spirit affecting the Church of Christ and its related community.

Dr. J. Edwin Orr

There is no revival without repentance.

Revival is not imported from the outside; it must begin on the inside.

Acts 3:19,20 Repent therefore, and turn again, that your sins may be blotted out, that times of refreshing may come from the presence of the Lord . . .

Psalm 85:6 Will you not revive us again, that your people may rejoice in you?

Notes:

September 22nd

Salvation

Salvation is necessary because sin against the Holy God separates us from Him, bringing judgement and spiritual death.

Salvation is the offer of divine forgiveness and the gift of eternal life (conversion is the way we enter into that experience and receive the gift).

Psalm 37:39 The salvation of the righteous is from the LORD; he is their stronghold in the time of trouble.

1 Thess. 5:9 For God has not destined us for wrath, but to obtain salvation through our Lord Jesus Christ . . .

1 Chron. 16:23 Sing to the LORD, all the earth! Tell of his salvation from day to day.

Notes:

Salvation

At conversion we are saved from the penalty of sin.

The Father plans salvation, the Son executes it and the Spirit administers it.

Salvation is the basis on which God establishes a relationship with his people.

Isaiah 61:10 I will greatly rejoice in the LORD; my soul shall exult in my God, for he has clothed me with the garments of salvation;

Psalm 27:1 The LORD is my light and my salvation; whom shall I fear?

Phil. 2:12 Therefore, my beloved, as you have always obeyed, so now, not only as in my (Paul's) presence but much more in my absence, work out your own salvation with fear and trembling . . .

Notes:

September 24th

Salvation

Day by day we are being saved from the power of sin and one day we will be saved from the presence of sin.

If God doesn't save us from something, it means he will save us in it.

Hebrews 2:10 For it was fitting that he (Jesus), . . . should make the founder of their salvation perfect through suffering.

Rev. 7:9,10 . . . a great multitude . . . crying out with a loud voice, "Salvation belongs to our God who sits on the throne, and to the Lamb!"

Psalm 13:5 But I (David) have trusted in your steadfast love; my heart shall rejoice in your salvation.

Notes:

Salvation

Salvation is not a licence to behave as we like, but liberty to freely do God's will.

Salvation is free, but discipleship will cost you everything you have. *Billy Graham*

Our salvation was forethought, foreseen and foreordained. We were saved in eternity.

---

2 Samuel 22:47 The LORD lives, and blessed be my rock, and exalted be my God, the rock of my salvation . . .

2 Tim. 3:15 . . . and you remember that ever since you were a child, you have known the Holy Scriptures, which are able to give you the wisdom that leads to salvation through faith in Christ Jesus. GNB.

Exodus 15:2 The LORD is my strength and my song, and he has become my salvation;

Notes:

September 26th

Salvation

"Today is the day of salvation." Many dream of tomorrow's faith and tomorrow's repentance, but find tomorrow never comes and death does not wait forever.

A prayer – Dear Lord, help me never to take my salvation for granted. It cost me nothing but you everything.

Romans 1:16 For I am not ashamed of the gospel, for it is the power of God for salvation to everyone who believes . . .

1 Peter 2:2 Like newborn infants, long for the pure spiritual milk, that by it you may grow up to salvation –

2 Cor. 7:10 For godly grief produces a repentance that leads to salvation without regret, whereas worldly grief produces death.

Notes:

Salvation

One thief was saved so no one need to despair, but only one, so no one should dare to presume.

God accepts us as we are, but when he accepts us, we cannot remain as we are. *Walter Trobisch*

Salvation is not something I achieve, but something I receive.

Micah 7:7 But as for me, I will look to the LORD; I will wait for the God of my salvation; my God will hear me.

Psalm 95:1 Oh come, let us sing to the LORD; let us make a joyful noise to the rock of our salvation!

Romans 10:13 For "everyone who calls on the name of the Lord will be saved."

Notes:

September 28th

Salvation

Salvation is the redemption of the individual from sin into eternal life through faith in a crucified, risen redeemer.

God thought it, Christ bought it, the Holy Spirit wrought it – thank God I've got it!

Christ saves from the guttermost to the uttermost.

Hebrews 5:9 And being made perfect, he (Jesus) became the source of eternal salvation to all who obey him . . .

Psalm 140:7 O Lord, my Lord, the strength of my salvation . . .

Psalm 118:14 The Lord is my strength and my song; he has become my salvation.

Notes:

Sanctify

Sanctification means to be set apart for God's use and to be made fit for God's use.

Sanctification comes through submission and surrender to Christ and remains as long as we stay submitted and surrendered to Christ. *Selwyn Hughes*

Hebrews 10:14 For by a single offering he (Jesus) has perfected for all time those who are being sanctified.

Romans 6:19 In the same way you must now surrender yourselves entirely as slaves of righteousness for holy purposes. GNB.

Notes:

September 30th

Sanctify

Sanctification is to be set apart from the world and being set apart to God.

Sanctification makes me one with Jesus Christ, and in Him one with God and it is done only through the superb Atonement of Christ. *Oswald Chambers*

John 17:16,17 They (God's people) are not of the world, just as I (Jesus) am not of the world. Sanctify them in the truth; your word is truth.

1 Thess. 4:3 For this is the will of God, your sanctification:

1 Cor. 6:11 And such were some of you. But you were washed, you were sanctified, you were justified in the name of the Lord Jesus Christ and by the Spirit of our God.

Notes:

Sanctify

Sanctification is an on-going process – it takes time to make a saint.

To sanctify means to be set apart, being made righteous. To be set apart for a particular purpose, to be special and distinctive.

To sanctify is to be cleansed from our sin.

Hebrews 10:10 And by that (God's) will we have been sanctified through the offering of the body of Jesus Christ once for all.

Hebrews 13:12 So Jesus also suffered outside the gate in order to sanctify the people through his own blood.

Notes:

October 2nd

Sanctify

Sanctification is a work of God in which He deals with the power and pollution of sin. He does so by infusing holiness into the soul.

We have been sanctified, we are being sanctified and someday we shall fully be sanctified.

---

1 Thess. 5:23 Now may the God of peace himself sanctify you completely, and may your whole spirit and soul and body be kept blameless at the coming of our Lord Jesus Christ.

Acts 20:32 And now I (Paul) commend you to God and to the word of his grace, which is able to build you up and to give you the inheritance among all those who are sanctified.

Notes:

Sin

Sin is deliberate violation, either by thought or action, of what we know to be right and true in our heart and conscience. Sin is breaking God's moral laws.

Floyd McClung

Sin is meant to be the exception and not the rule.

---

1 John 1:7 But if we walk in the light, as he (God) is in the light, we have fellowship with one another, and the blood of Jesus his Son cleanses us from all sin.

2 Chron. 7:14 . . . if my people who are called by my name humble themselves, and pray and seek my face and turn from their wicked ways, then I will hear from heaven and will forgive their sin and heal their land.

Notes:

October 4th

Sin

There are two types of sin. One is doing what we know to be wrong: the other is not doing what we know to be right.

We are free to sin, but not to choose the consequences.

Sin is the collision of a created will with the will of the Creator.

Matthew 12:31 Therefore I (Jesus) tell you, every sin and blasphemy will be forgiven people, but the blasphemy against the Spirit will not be forgiven.

Psalm 119:11 I have stored up your word in my heart, that I might not sin against you.

Notes:

Sin

The nature of sin is forsaking the Lord as our God; it is the soul's alienation from Him, and aversion to Him.

Matthew Henry

Sin is the ego in the place where God wants to be.

Does God's effort to render inoperative the energy of sin mean it is not possible to sin again? No, but it is possible not to sin.

Psalm 32:1 Happy are those whose sins are forgiven, whose wrongs are pardoned. GNB.

John 1:29 The next day he (John) saw Jesus coming towards him, and said, "Behold, the Lamb of God, who takes away the sin of the world!"

Notes:

October 6th

Sin

Sin is a master who pays his slaves with death.

Within my earthly temple, there's a crowd,
There's one of us that's humble; one that's proud.
There's one that's broken-hearted for his sins,
And one who unrepentant, sits and grins.

Sanford Martin

(Continued tomorrow)

Ecclesiastes 7:20 Surely there is not a righteous man on earth who does good and never sins.

1 Cor. 15:3 For I (Paul) delivered to you as of first importance what I also received: that Christ died for our sins in accordance with the Scriptures . . .

Notes:

Sin

(Continued from yesterday)

There's one who loves his neighbour as himself,
And one who cares for nought but fame and self,
From much corroding care would I be free,
If once I could determine which is me.

Sanford Martin

Sin is making oneself the centre of the universe.

William Temple

---

1 John 3:5 You know that he (Jesus) appeared to take away sins, and in him there is no sin.

Psalm 51:1,2,3 Have mercy on me, O God, according to your steadfast love; according to your abundant mercy blot out my transgressions. Wash me thoroughly from my iniquity, and cleanse me from my sin! For I know my transgressions, and my sin is ever before me.

Notes:

October 8th

Sin

We sin because we are wrong; sinning doesn't make us wrong.

We are not sinners because we sin, but rather we sin because we are sinners.

God isn't against us for our sin, but for us against our sin.

The root of sin is the suspicion that God is not good.

---

1 John 2:1 My little children, I am writing these things to you so that you may not sin. But if anyone does sin, we have an advocate with the Father, Jesus Christ the righteous.

1 Peter 2:22 He (Jesus) committed no sin, neither was deceit found in his mouth.

Notes:

Sin

A good description of sin is Isaiah 53:6. All we like sheep have gone astray; we have turned every one to his own way.
A. W. Tozer

God's word will keep you from sin, or sin will keep you form God's word.

Sin is a declaration of independence; an attempt to do for ourselves what only God can do for us.

---

2 Cor. 5:21 For our sake he made him (Jesus) to be sin who knew no sin, so that in him we might become the righteousness of God.

Psalm 66:18 If I had cherished iniquity in my heart, the Lord would not have listened.

Notes:

Sin

No one can say, "I cannot sin", but a Christian can say, "I need not sin".

Christ paid the penalty of sin, yet chastisement and correction may still be laid on us.

Sin is failure to glorify God.

Sin is missing the mark.

Proverbs 28:13 Whoever conceals his transgressions will not prosper, but he who confesses and forsakes them will obtain mercy.

1 Cor. 15:56,57 Death gets its power to hurt from sin, and sin gets its power from the Law. But thanks be to God who gives us the victory through our Lord Jesus Christ! GNB.

Notes:

Sin

The more a decision will affect your way of life, the more your sinful nature will enter the debate.

Sin is disharmony with the moral nature and purpose of God as revealed in Christ. *Halford Luccok*

Sin is . . . I will.

Romans 6:6 And we know that our old being has been put to death with Christ on his cross, in order that the power of the sinful self might be destroyed, so that we should no longer be the slaves of sin. GNB.

1 Peter 3:18 For Christ also suffered once for sins, the righteous for the unrighteous, that he might bring us to God . . .

Notes:

October 12th

Sin

Sin is the consciousness of the lack of God.

I am against sin. I'll kick it as long as I have a foot.
I'll fight it as long as I have a fist.
I'll butt it as long as I've got a head.

Billy Sunday

(Continued tomorrow)

Matthew 1:21 She (Mary) will have a son, and you will name him Jesus – because he will save his people from their sins. GNB.

Romans 6:11 So you also must consider yourselves dead to sin and alive to God in Christ Jesus.

Notes:

Sin

(Continued from yesterday)

I'll bite it as long as I've got a tooth.
And when I'm old and fistless and footless and toothless,
I'll gum it until I go home to glory and it goes home to perdition.

Billy Sunday

First we practise sin, then defend it, then boast of it.

Thomas Mann

---

1 John 3:4 Whoever sins is guilty of breaking God's law, because sin is a breaking of the law. GNB.

Romans 6:23 For the wages of sin is death, but the free gift of God is eternal life in Christ Jesus our Lord.

Notes:

October 14th

Sin

Sin will take you further than you wanted to go.
It will keep you longer than you wanted to stay.
It will cost you more than you intended to pay.

A little sin is like being a little pregnant. It will eventually show itself. *Rick Warren*

Isaiah 43:25 And yet, I am the God who forgives your sins, and I do this because of who I am. I will not hold your sins against you. GNB.

James 4:17 So whoever knows the right thing to do and fails to do it, for him it is sin.

Notes:

Sin

Let a man really understand the sinfulness of sin and the mercy of the Lord in dying for Him, and he will never think anything too great a sacrifice for his Lord.

Sin stops us from contact with God.

Sin is God's one great intolerance.

Hebrews 9:28 . . . so Christ, having been offered once to bear the sins of many, will appear a second time, not to deal with sin but to save those who are eagerly waiting for him.

1 Peter 2:24 He (Jesus) himself bore our sins in his body on the tree, that we might die to sin and live to righteousness. By his wounds you have been healed.

Notes:

October 16th

Sin

Though we can never reach a point in this life where it is not possible to sin, we can have a relationship with Christ through which it becomes possible not to sin.

When sin is tolerated, it increases.

Sin is a stubborn refusal to deal with truth.

---

1 John 1:8,9 If we say we have no sin, we deceive ourselves, and the truth is not in us. If we confess our sins, he is faithful and just to forgive our sins and to cleanse us from all unrighteousness.

Romans 8:10 But if Christ is in you, although the body is dead because of sin, the Spirit is life because of righteousness.

Notes:

Sin

Sin is shaking a fist in God's face and saying, "I want to run my life on my own terms."

The awful thing about sin is not so much that we break God's law, but that we break His heart.

Romans 3:23 . . . for all have sinned and fall short of the glory of God . . .

Rev. 1:5,6 He (Jesus) loves us, and by his sacrificial death he has freed us from our sins and made us a kingdom of priests to serve his God and Father. GNB.

Notes:

October 18th

Sin

Sin is that which takes Jesus, who was incarnate God, treats Him as no beast should be treated, strips Him, lashes Him, pierces Him with nails, hangs Him on a tree and then laughs at Him. That is sin. Your sin, and mine. *Selwyn Hughes*

James 1:15 Then desire when it has conceived gives birth to sin, and sin when it is fully grown brings forth death.

Gal. 1:4 In order to set us free from this present evil age, Christ gave himself for our sins, in obedience to the will of our God and Father. GNB.

Notes:

Sin

God in heaven holds each person by a string. When we sin, we cut the string. Then God ties it up again, making a knot – and thereby bringing us a little closer to himself.

Sin is deadly serious.

We cannot win heaven and wear sin. *C. H. Spurgeon*

Isaiah 1:18 "Come now, let us reason together, says the LORD: though your sins are like scarlet, they shall be as white as snow; though they are red like crimson, they shall become like wool."

Matthew 18:15 "If your brother sins against you, go to him and show him his fault. But do it privately, just between yourselves." GNB.

Notes:

October 20th

Sin

We are all descended from a dishonest gardener who stole his master's fruit.

We cannot continue in a sinful situation, even if we did not initiate it. Simple acknowledgement and confession is not sufficient, something must be done.

Sin is a violation of the law of love.

Psalm 32:5 I acknowledged my sin to you, and I did not cover my iniquity; I said, "I will confess my transgressions to the LORD", and you forgave the iniquity of my sin.

Hebrews 3:13 But exhort one another every day, as long as it is called "today", that none of you may be hardened by the deceitfulness of sin.

Notes:

Sin

Sin is the resistance movement that runs in our nature and is hostile towards God.

Sin is a human will colliding with the divine will.

A Christian can fall into sin, but he or she does not belong in sin.

Matthew 26:27,28 And he (Jesus) took a cup, and when he had given thanks he gave it to them (the disciples), saying, "Drink of it, all of you, for this is my blood of the covenant, which is poured out for many for the forgiveness of sins."

John 8:34 Jesus answered them, "Truly, truly, I say to you, everyone who commits sin is a slave to sin."

Notes:

October 22nd

Soul

The soul is the ability to understand with the mind and senses and put what is perceived into a frame of reference.

The soul is the seat of emotions, feelings, the will, the conscious, intellect, thoughts, desires, mentality, personality, etc.

The soul can never be satisfied with anything less than God.

Matthew 22:36,37 "Teacher, which is the great commandment in the Law?" And he (Jesus) said to him (a lawyer), "You shall love the Lord your God with all your heart and with all your soul and with all your mind."

Notes:

Submission

An African Christian said being submitted to God is like a needle and thread. He is the needle, I am the thread. He goes first and where He leads, I follow.

Gal. 5:1 Freedom is what we have – Christ has set us free! Stand, then, as free people, and do not allow yourselves to become slaves again. GNB.

Titus 3:1 Remind them (your people) to be submissive to rulers and authorities, to be obedient, to be ready for every good work . . .

Luke 2:51 And he (Jesus) went down with them (His parents) and came to Nazareth and was submissive to them.

Notes:

October 24th

Submission

Submission is to submit to instruction as well as correction from other believers; to be teachable or to be humble enough to admit we have erred when other believers correct us. *J. Bridges*

The whole of life after submission is a continuous desire for communion with God.

Romans 8:7 For the mind that is set on the flesh is hostile to God, for it does not submit to God's law;

Hebrews 13:17 Obey your leaders and submit to them, for they are keeping watch over your souls . . .

James 4:7 Submit yourselves therefore to God.

Notes:

Success

A prayer – O God, whilst I long to be successful in everything I turn my hand to, help me, however, not to be in bondage to success. Help me always do that which is right and submit to the outcome whatever it may be.

Psalm 84:11 No good thing does he (God) withhold from those who walk uprightly.

1 Samuel 18:14 And David had success in all his undertakings, for the LORD was with him.

Notes:

October 26th

Suffering

The Christian life does not promise exemption from injustice and suffering, but it does promise power to make something good out of everything that happens.

Selwyn Hughes

We are not kept from suffering; we are kept in it

Matthew 16:21 From that time Jesus began to show his disciples that he must go to Jerusalem and suffer many things . . .

Acts 5:41 Then they (the apostles) left the presence of the council, rejoicing that they were counted worthy to suffer dishonour for the name.

Psalm 31:7 I will be glad and rejoice because of your constant love. You see my suffering; you know my trouble. GNB.

Notes:

Suffering

I'm convinced that the path of every believer will sooner or later include suffering. *Brother Yun*

What counts is not so much what we suffer, but how we react to what we suffer.

God only allows what He can use.

Luke 24:26 Was it not necessary that the Christ should suffer these things and enter into his glory?

1 Peter 2:21 For to this you have been called, because Christ also suffered for you, leaving you an example, so that you might follow in his steps.

John 14:1 Let not your hearts be troubled. Believe in God; believe also in me (Jesus).

Notes:

October 28th

Suffering

Suffering is never beneficial in itself and must always be fought against. What makes it beneficial are the lessons one is able to draw from it.

Suffering is to be redemptive; sickness is to be healed.

Sometimes God upsets us in order to set us up.

---

2 Cor. 1:3,4,5 Blessed be the God and Father of our Lord Jesus Christ, the Father of mercies and God of all comfort, who comforts us in all our affliction, so that we may be able to comfort those who are in affliction, with the comfort with which we ourselves are comforted by God. For as we share abundantly in Christ's sufferings, so through Christ we share abundantly in comfort too.

Notes:

Suffering

When God puts a tear in your eye, it's because He wants to put a rainbow in your heart.

His purposes will ripen fast,
unfolding every hour,
the bud may have a bitter taste,
but sweet will be the flower.

W. Cowper

Hebrew 2:10 For it was fitting that he, for whom and by whom all things exist, in bringing many sons to glory, should make the founder of their salvation perfect through suffering.

Romans 5:3 More than that, we rejoice in our sufferings, knowing that suffering produces endurance . . .

Phil. 1:29 For it has been granted to you that for the sake of Christ you should not only believe in him but also suffer for his sake . . .

Notes:

October 30th

Suffering

When suffering:

1. Review your confidence in God.
2. Pray earnestly, definitely and believingly.
3. Count your blessings.
4. Saturate yourself with God's word.
5. Praise the Lord.
6. Forget yourself and love others.
7. Submit yourself totally to God.

Theodore Epp

---

1 Peter 4:16 Yet if anyone suffers as a Christian, let him not be ashamed, but let him glorify God in that name.

Romans 8:18 For I consider that the sufferings of this present time are not worth comparing with the glory that is to be revealed to us.

1 Peter 5:7 Leave all your worries with him (Jesus), because he cares for you. GNB.

Notes:

Temptation

The reasons that Christians fall into sin is that they treat temptation like strawberry shortcake rather than a rattlesnake.

Billy Sunday

Our test can be our testimony.

Temptation is not a sin, unless we yield to it.

Gal. 6:1 Brothers, if anyone is caught in any transgression, you who are spiritual should restore him in a spirit of gentleness. Keep watch on yourself, lest you too be tempted.

Matthew 6:13 And lead us not into temptation . . .

Notes:

November 1st

Temptation

The captain of a ship does not sail near to the rocks simply to investigate them, he avoids them and keeps as far away as possible.

How often Satan leads us gently down the slope, when we would fear jumping from the cliff.

Matthew 18:7 "Woe to the world for temptations to sin! For it is necessary that temptations come, but woe to the one by whom the temptation comes!"

1 Tim. 6:9 But those who desire to be rich fall into temptation . . .

2 Peter 2:9 And so the Lord knows how to rescue godly people from their trials . . . GNB.

Notes:

Temptation

No one can honestly ask to be delivered from temptation, unless he has honestly and firmly determined to do the best he can to keep out of it. *John Ruskin*

Five points to overcome temptation (James 4):

1. Submit to God.
2. Resist the devil.
3. Come near to God.
4. Wash your hands
5. Purify your heart.

Hebrews 4:15 For we do not have a high priest who is unable to sympathize with our weaknesses, but one who in every respect has been tempted as we are, yet without sin.

Matthew 26:41 Watch and pray that you may not enter into temptation. The spirit is willing, but the flesh is weak.

Notes:

November 3rd

Temptation

Temptation is not only an encouragement to do wrong, but also a trial or testing.

The devil doesn't work overtime, he works all the time.

You cannot stop the crows flying over your head, but you can stop them nesting in your hair. *Billy Bray*

James 1:13,14 Let no one say when he is tempted, "I am being tempted by God", for God cannot be tempted with evil, and he himself tempts no one. But each person is tempted when he is lured and enticed by his own desire.

Notes:

Temptation

Temptation is to beguile to do wrong, by promise of pleasure or gain.

God will not deliver us from temptation, but He will deliver us in it, i.e. He will supply us with the grace to overcome it.

1 Cor. 10:13 No temptation has overtaken you that is not common to man. God is faithful, and he will not let you be tempted beyond your ability, but with the temptation he will also provide the way of escape, that you may be able to endure it.

Hebrews 2:18 For because he himself (Jesus) has suffered when tempted, he is able to help those who are being tempted.

Notes:

November 5th

Temptation

The purpose behind every temptation which God allows is the development of character. *Selwyn Hughes*

Temptation motivates you to be bad, by promising something good.

Temptation is an enticement to act independently of God.

Matthew 4:1 Then Jesus was led up by the Spirit into the wilderness to be tempted by the devil.

James 1:2,3 My brothers and sisters, consider yourselves fortunate when all kinds of trials come your way, for you know that when your faith succeeds in facing such trials, the result is the ability to endure. GNB.

Notes:

Time

God's time is always the right time.

How long you've been a Christian only tells how long you've been on the road – it doesn't tell how far you've come.

All that is not eternal, is eternally out of date. *C. S. Lewis*

Romans 5:6 For when we were still helpless, Christ died for the wicked at the time that God chose. GNB.

Ecclesiastes 3:11 He has made everything beautiful in it's time.

Notes:

November 7th

Time

Regard your time as His time.

To make better use of your time:

1. Start the day with the Lord.
2. Plan your day.
3. Take "blessing breaks" during the day – brief times of praise and prayer for the purpose of quietening the heart and getting new guidance and strength from the Lord.

Warren Wiersbe

(Continued tomorrow)

James 4:14 . . . What is your life? For you are a mist that appears for a little time and then vanishes.

Genesis 2:2 And on the seventh day God finished his work that he had done, and he rested on the seventh day from all his work that he had done.

Notes:

Time

(Continued from yesterday)

4. Try to keep "margins" around your life. Don't practise brinkmanship and stay ahead on long-range projects.
5. Live to please God and fulfil his purpose for you.
6. Learn to relax and enjoy leisure time.

Warren Wiersbe

Beware of the barrenness of a busy life. *Fred Mitchell*

Psalm 121:8 The LORD will keep your going out and your coming in from this time forth and for evermore.

Gal. 4:4 But when the fullness of time had come, God sent forth his Son . . .

Notes:

November 9th

Time

Not till the loom is silent and the shuttles cease
to fly,
Shall God unroll the canvas and explain the
reason why,
The dark threads are as needful in the weaver's
skilful hand,
As the threads of gold and silver in the pattern
He has planned.

Time is distilled opportunity.

Acts 1:7 Jesus said to them, (the apostles), "The times and occasions are set by my Father's own authority, and it is not for you to know when they will be." GNB.

Proverbs 27:1 Do not boast about tomorrow, for you do not know what a day may bring.

Notes:

Time

If you do not wish to be full of regrets when you are obliged to be still, work while you can. If you desire to make your sickbed as soft as can be, do not stuff it with mournful reflection that you wasted time while you were in health and strength. *C. H. Spurgeon*

Ecclesiastes 12:1 Remember also your Creator in the days of your youth . . .

Psalm 90:12 Teach us how short our life is, so that we may become wise. GNB.

Col. 4:5 Conduct yourselves wisely towards outsiders, making the best use of the time.

Notes:

November 11th

Time

Life depends not on the hours you put in, but what you put into the hours. Wait for the days and months to speak against the hours.

There are certain things in life for which we must make time. Time to think, pray, talk and do nothing.

William Barclay

Eph. 5:15,16 Look carefully then how you walk, not as unwise but as wise, making the best use of the time, because the days are evil.

Ecclesiastes 3:1 For everything there is a season, and a time for every matter under heaven;

2 Peter 3:8 But do not forget one thing, my dear friends! There is no difference in the Lord's sight between one day and a thousand years; to him the two are the same. GNB.

Notes:

Tongue

Six ways to help you tame the tongue:

1. Dedicate your heart and your tongue to the Lord daily.
2. Assume responsibility for every word you speak.
3. Ask those around you what offensive words you use.
4. Learn how to use words that encourage, edify, comfort and inspire.
5. Ask a person's forgiveness every time you offend them with wrong words.
6. Urge your friends to tell you when you offend them by your words.

Selwyn Hughes

---

1 Peter 3:10 For "Whoever desires to love life and see good days, let him keep his tongue from evil and his lips from speaking deceit;"

Notes:

November 13th

Trinity

One God who is three separate persons: co-equal, co-eternal and co-existent.

All the members of the Trinity have a special function to perform. The Father manifests love, the Son manifests light and the Holy Spirit manifests life. *Selwyn Hughes*

---

1 John 5:7,8 For there are three that testify: the Spirit and the water and the blood; and these three agree.

Matthew 28:19 Go therefore and make disciples of all nations, baptizing them in the name of the Father and of the Son and of the Holy Spirit . . .

Notes:

Trinity

God is one but with three distinct centres of consciousness.

God is one, yet God is three. How can such a strange thing be?

We may not understand the Trinity, but those who have the mind of Christ bow before it in reverence, amazement and worship.

John 15:26 "The Helper will come – the Spirit, who reveals the truth about God and who comes from the Father. I (Jesus) will send him to you from the Father, and he will speak about me." GNB.

2 Cor. 13:14 The grace of the Lord Jesus Christ and the love of God and the fellowship of the Holy Spirit be with you all.

Notes:

November 15th

Trust

You need to trust Jesus Christ as your saviour, not only because you may die tonight, but also because you may have to live tomorrow.

The closer you get to God, the less you understand Him, but the more you trust Him. *Selwyn Hughes*

Psalm 62:8 Trust in him at all times, O people; pour out your heart before him; God is a refuge for us.

Jeremiah 17:7 Blessed is the man who trusts in the LORD, whose trust is the LORD.

Psalm 84:12 O LORD of hosts, blessed is the one who trusts in you!

Notes:

Trust

We trust as if it all depended on God, and we work as if it all depended on us. *C. H. Spurgeon*

Trust is confidence that what we believe about a person is true.

Trust in God, and keep your powder dry.
Oliver Cromwell

Trust is accepting only those responsibilities God intends us to have.

Proverbs 28:25 A greedy man stirs up strife, but the one who trusts in the LORD will be enriched.

Proverbs 3:5 Trust in the LORD with all your heart, and do not lean on your own understanding.

Notes:

November 17th

Trust

Trust is a condition of the heart that gives us the freedom to ask what we desire, but to remain completely content with whatever comes – so long as we have the promise that our Father is there.

God is to be trusted when His providences seem to run contrary to his promises. *Thomas Watson*

Isaiah 12:2 "Behold, God is my salvation; I will trust, and will not be afraid;"

Psalm 118:8 It is better to take refuge in the LORD than to trust in man.

Isaiah 26:4 Trust in the LORD for ever; he will always protect us. GNB.

Notes:

Trust

Trust means believing God is in control of one's life and that He is constantly working to ensure His purposes are brought to pass – even through our mistakes and foibles, and even in the midst of massive confusion and uncertainty.

Psalm 56:3 When I am afraid, I put my trust in you.

Psalm 37:5 Give yourself to the LORD; trust in him, and he will help you; GNB.

Psalm 32:10 Many are the sorrows of the wicked, but steadfast love surrounds the one who trusts in the LORD.

Notes:

November 19th

Truth

Truth is like a portrait and to exaggerate one feature is to turn the portrait into a caricature.

The neglect of truth, followed by its re-discovery, often results in overemphasis.

Faithful witness is truth telling, not head counting.

John 14:6 Jesus said to him (Thomas), "I am the way, and the truth, and the life. No one comes to the Father except through me."

Eph. 4:25 No more lying, then! Each of you must tell the truth to one another, because we are all members together in the body of Christ. GNB.

Notes:

Truth

We may have a good grasp of the truth, but has the truth grasped us?

A lie will travel halfway around the world before the truth can get its boots on. *Billy Sunday*

Truth out of context can soon become error.

Everyone loves the truth, but not everyone tells it.

John 8:31,32 So Jesus said to those who believed in him, "If you obey my teaching, you are really my disciples; you will know the truth, and the truth will set you free." GNB.

1 Cor. 13:6 . . . it (love) . . . rejoices with the truth.

Notes:

November 21st

Truth

Christians are losing the world with the truth; others are winning it with a lie.

If we do not heed the truth, then we do not hear the truth.

The greatest truths are not just spoken, but acted.

John 16:13 When the Spirit of truth comes, he will guide you into all the truth . . .

Psalm 86:11 Teach me your way, O LORD, that I may walk in your truth;

1 John 1:8 If we say we have no sin, we deceive ourselves, and the truth is not in us.

Notes:

Truth

The truth of God should bring us to the God of truth.

Truth must be bought and those who are unwilling to pay the price must go without it.

All truth is important, but not all truth is equally important.

Proverbs 23:23 Truth, wisdom, learning, and good sense – these are worth paying for, but too valuable for you to sell. GNB.

1 Tim. 2:3,4 . . . God our Saviour, who desires all people to be saved and to come to the knowledge of the truth.

John 17:17 Sanctify them in the truth; your (God's) word is truth.

Notes:

November 23rd

Unbelief

Unbelief is a wilful refusal to believe, resulting in a deliberate decision to disobey. It is a state of mind which is closed against God, an attitude of heart which disobeys God as much as it disbelieves the truth. It is the consequence of a settled choice. *Selwyn Hughes*

Matthew 13:58 And he (Jesus) did not do many mighty works there, because of their unbelief.

Mark 9:23,24 And Jesus said to him, "If you can! All things are possible for one who believes." Immediately the father of the child cried out and said, "I believe; help my unbelief!"

Notes:

Unbelief

Unbelief expects nothing and gets it.

Distinguish between two kinds of unbelief: rejection of the truth when it is first presented, and more seriously, after it has been professed. *Hugo Grotius*

Don't dig up in unbelief what you have sown in faith.

Mark 16:14 Afterwards he (Jesus) appeared to the eleven themselves as they were reclining at table, and he rebuked them for their unbelief and hardness of heart, because they had not believed those who saw him after he had risen.

Notes:

Unity

Unity is not unanimity (being of the same mind about everything) or uniformity (everyone looking the same as each other or worshipping in the same way). Unity comes from power within, uniformity from pressure without.

Unity without diversity leads to uniformity.

Warren Wiersbe

John 17:21 I (Jesus) pray that they may all be one. Father! May they be in us, just as you are in me and I am in you. May they be one, so that the world will believe that you sent me. GNB.

Psalm 133:1 Behold, how good and pleasant it is when brothers dwell in unity!

Notes:

Unity

1. Unity is the sense of being one with the Father and one with all the Father's other children.
2. Unity is the willingness to demonstrate a strong and vigorous love to all those other children – a love that crosses all boundaries, all barriers and all lives.

Selwyn Hughes

(Continued tomorrow)

Romans 15:5,6 And may God, the source of patience and encouragement, enable you to have the same point of view among yourselves by following the example of Christ Jesus, so that all of you together may praise with one voice the God and Father of our Lord Jesus Christ. GNB.

Romans 12:16 Live in harmony with one another.

Notes:

November 27th

Unity

(Continued from yesterday)

3. Unity means that when we fail in love, we drop on our knees and put it right before God, and, if necessary, with any brother or sister we have wronged.
4. Unity means disagreeing without being disagreeable, forgiving one another and seeking reconciliation.

Selwyn Hughes

---

1 Cor. 10:17 Because there is one bread, we who are many are one body, for we all partake of the one bread.

1 Peter 3:8 Finally, all of you, have unity of mind, sympathy, brotherly love, a tender heart, and a humble mind.

Notes:

Unity

Wherever there is spiritual unity there will be freedom and diversity. Wherever there is uniformity there will be bondage and conformity.

In essentials, unity; in non-essentials, liberty; in all things, charity.
St. Augustine

Unity is like a wheel; the nearer the hub, the nearer the spokes together.

---

1 Cor. 1:10 By the authority of our Lord Jesus Christ I appeal to all of you, my brothers and sisters, to agree in what you say, so that there will be no divisions among you. Be completely united, with only one thought and one purpose. GNB.

Notes:

November 29th

Unity

Unity is the bond that exists between one person and another in which they know that the things that unite them are deeper and more important than the things that might separate them. *Selwyn Hughes*

Do not seek unity, but maintain it.

Phil. 2:2 . . . complete my (Paul's) joy by being of the same mind, having the same love, being in full accord and of one mind.

Romans 12:5 In the same way, though we are many, we are one body in union with Christ, and we are all joined to each other as different parts of one body. GNB.

2 Cor. 13:11 Finally, brothers, . . . agree with one another, live in peace;

Notes:

Will

There is God's sovereign will – a predetermined plan for all ages and is always fulfilled.

There is God's moral will – revealed in the Scriptures e.g. how to live.

There is God's individual will – the ideal detailed life plan for every believer.

---

1 Thess. 4:3 For this is the will of God, your sanctification:

Psalm 143:10 You are my God; teach me to do your will. GNB.

Matthew 7:21 "Not everyone who says to me, 'Lord, Lord', will enter the kingdom of heaven, but the one who does the will of my Father who is in heaven."

Notes:

December 1st

Will

God repeats situations in our lives until we learn the lessons they are meant to teach us.

Doing the will of God leaves me no time for disputing about His plans. *George MacDonald*

Those who take God's way get results; those who don't get consequences.

Matthew 26:39 And going a little farther he (Jesus) fell on his face and prayed, saying, "My Father, if it be possible, let this cup pass from me; nevertheless, not as I will, but as you will."

Notes:

Will

The shattering of our plans is but the prelude to the advancement of His.

Many things appear irretrievable to us, but there is nothing irretrievable with God. *Thomas Erskine*

There is always enough time to do and enjoy all that God has for us.

Matthew 26:42 Once more Jesus went away and prayed, "My Father, if this cup of suffering cannot be taken away unless I drink it, your will be done." GNB.

Hebrews 13:20,21 Now may the God of peace . . . equip you with everything good that you may do his will . . .

Notes:

December 3rd

Will

Prosperity means having enough to do the will of God.

O Lord, grant that I may do Thy will as if it were my will, so that thou mayest do my will, as if it were Thy will.

St. Augustine

God only allows what He can use.

Rev. 4:11 "Worthy are you, our Lord and God, to receive glory and honour and power, for you created all things, and by your will they existed and were created."

Eph. 5:17 Therefore do not be foolish, but understand what the will of the Lord is.

Notes:

Will

It is not success that God rewards, but the faithfulness of doing His will.

It is better for us to be poor and hungry in the will of God, than to have all the comforts of life apart from the will of God. *Warren Wiersbe*

John 6:38 For I (Jesus) have come down from heaven, not to do my own will but the will of him who sent me.

Matthew 12:50 "For whoever does the will of my Father in heaven is my brother and sister and mother."

Notes:

December 5th

Will

My will is my ruin, God's will is my release.

Selwyn Hughes

Jesus knew that nothing could happen to Him without God permitting it, and that everything God permitted, He would use.

God does not make known His will to us that the knowledge of it may perish with us. *John Calvin*

Matthew 6:10 Your kingdom come, your will be done, on earth as it is in heaven.

Romans 12:2 Do not conform yourselves to the standards of this world, but let God transform you inwardly by a complete change of your mind. Then you will be able to know the will of God – what is good and is pleasing to him and is perfect. GNB.

Notes:

Will

There is a far greater danger of missing God's will by sitting still than by moving.

God's will must take precedence over God's work.

The divine attention to detail is amazing; nothing is too trivial for omnipotence. *Samuel Chadwick*

1 Peter 3:17 For it is better to suffer for doing good, if this should be God's will, than for doing evil. GNB.

1 Thess. 5:16,17,18 Rejoice always, pray without ceasing, give thanks in all circumstances; for this is the will of God in Christ Jesus for you.

Notes:

Will

I belong with my feet on the earth and the Spirit of God in my heart, walking straight up to the task that God has called me to do. *Selwyn Hughes*

Decisions can take you out of God's will, but never out of His reach.

---

1 John 5:14 We have courage in God's presence, because we are sure that he hears us if we ask him for anything that is according to his will. GNB.

Psalm 40:8 I desire to do your will, O my God; your law is within my heart.

Notes:

Wisdom

To have wisdom is to have the insight to know how to speak and act in a manner that honours God, when all sorts of pressures come upon us to dishonour Him.

Wisdom is the correct application of knowledge.

Proverbs 4:7,8,9 Getting wisdom is the most important thing you can do. Whatever else you get, get insight. Love wisdom, and she will make you great. Embrace her, and she will bring you honour. She will be your crowning glory. GNB.

Job 28:12,28 But where shall wisdom be found? . . . Behold, the fear of the Lord, that is wisdom . . .

Notes:

December 9th

Wisdom

Wisdom is the power to see, and the inclination to choose the best and highest goal, together with the surest means of attaining it. *J. I. Packer*

The principal part of wisdom is to know the Lord in an ultimate and personal way.

---

1 Cor. 1:30 But God has brought you into union with Christ Jesus, and God has made Christ to be our wisdom. GNB.

Proverbs 8:11 . . . for wisdom is better than jewels, and all that you may desire cannot compare with her.

Ecclesiastes 9:16 But I say that wisdom is better than might . . .

Notes:

Wisdom

Wisdom is to know the Lord, not just about Him.

Wisdom is seeing life from God's point of view.

The goal of divine wisdom is not to make us happy, but to make us Holy.

Wisdom is the ability to make right choices and sound decisions.

Proverbs 3:13 Blessed is the one who finds wisdom, and the one who gets understanding . . .

Jeremiah 10:12 The LORD made the earth by his power; by his wisdom he created the world and stretched out the heavens. GNB.

1 Cor. 3:19 For the wisdom of this world is folly with God.

Notes:

December 11th

Wisdom

Wisdom is the ability to forgive and to decide what is the best thing to do in any given situation.

Wisdom is an understanding and application of the moral principles of God. *J. Bridges*

Wisdom is to know God and to submit to His holiness and righteousness.

James 3:17 But the wisdom from above is pure first of all; it is also peaceful, gentle, and friendly; it is full of compassion and produces a harvest of good deeds; it is free from prejudice and hypocrisy. GNB.

Ecclesiastes 7:19 Wisdom does more for a person than ten rulers can do for a city. GNB.

Notes:

Wisdom

Wisdom has several distinguishing characteristics. It is:

1. Pure.
2. Gentle and willing to yield.
3. Peaceable.
4. Full of mercy and good fruits.
5. Without partiality.
6. Without hypocrisy.

Selwyn Hughes

Wisdom is the art of living a righteous life in this fallen world.

Psalm 104:24 O LORD, how manifold are your works! In wisdom have you made them all;

James 1:5 If any of you lacks wisdom, let him ask God . . . and it will be given him.

Notes:

December 13th

Wisdom

Man shows off his knowledge by flying faster than sound, but shows his lack of wisdom by going in the wrong direction.

A wise man is one who humbly seeks to discover the will of God.

Wisdom is the skill of living.

Col. 1:9 And so, from the day we heard, we have not ceased to pray for you, asking that you may be filled with the knowledge of his will in all spiritual wisdom and understanding . . .

Proverbs 2:6 For the LORD gives wisdom; from his mouth come knowledge and understanding;

Notes:

Work

What we are is more important than what we do, for the doing will come from the being.

We should not be concerned about working for God until we have learned the meaning and the delight of worshipping Him.

A. W. Tozer

Psalm 62:12 . . . For you (LORD) will render to a man according to his work.

Romans 12:11 Work hard and do not be lazy. Serve the Lord with a heart full of devotion. GNB.

Notes:

December 15th

Work

No matter the task ahead of you, it is never as great as the power behind you.

God respects me when I work, but he loves me when I sing.
R. Tagore

Not able to do it: but enabled to do it.

Do your best, commit the rest.

---

2 Thess. 3:11,12 For we hear that some among you walk in idleness, not busy at work, but busybodies. Now such persons we command and encourage in the Lord Jesus Christ to do their work quietly and to earn their own living.

Notes:

Work

It is critical that we stop doing the things that are urgent and start doing the things that are important.

J. Allen Peterson

Father, help me to remember that doing the right thing is always the right thing to do.

God's work, done in God's way, will never lack God's supply.
Hudson Taylor

Psalm 19:1 The heavens declare the glory of God, and the sky above proclaims his handiwork.

Jeremiah 48:10 Cursed is he who does the work of the LORD with slackness . . .

Col. 3:23 Whatever you do, work heartily, as for the Lord and not for men . . .

Notes:

December 17th

Work

God is more concerned about the worker, than He is about the work.

Do not be eager to work for God, but let God work through you.

When we do what we can, God will do what we can't.

---

2 Thess. 2:16,17 Now may our Lord Jesus Christ himself, and God our Father . . . comfort your hearts and establish them in every good work and word.

Exodus 23:12 For six days you shall do your work, but on the seventh day you shall rest;

Notes:

Work

Many Christians refuse to do anything because they cannot do everything. Because they cannot set the world on fire, they refuse to light a candle.

The supernatural is simply God adding His super to your natural.

Never be unemployed, and never fritter away time when employed.

John Wesley

---

2 Tim. 3:16,17 All Scripture is breathed out by God and profitable for teaching, for reproof, for correction, and for training in righteousness, that the man of God may be competent, equipped for every good work.

Notes:

December 19th

Work

If God hasn't given you an ability, he doesn't expect that responsibility.

The way to joy, peace and assurance is "to mind your work more than your wages." *Thomas Brooks*

We are created to be, as well as to do.

John 17:4 I (Jesus) have shown your (God's) glory on earth; I have finished the work you gave me to do. GNB.

Isaiah 64:8 But now, O LORD, you are our Father; we are the clay, and you are our potter; we are all the work of your hand.

Notes:

Work

Our actions must be governed not by what feels right, but what is right – not by our emotions, but by the word of God.

When we supply the willingness, God supplies the power.

A busy life is not necessarily a fruitful one.

Ecclesiastes 9:10 Whatever your hand finds to do, do it with your might . . .

Phil. 1:6 And so I am sure that God, who began this good work in you, will carry it on until it is finished on the Day of Christ Jesus. GNB.

Notes:

December 21st

Worry

Worry is a cycle of inefficient thought whirling around a centre of fear.

Worry is the ploughing up of endless possibilities.

Worry is a chronic process of making mountains out of molehills.

Worry: the antidote is faith.

---

1 Peter 5:7 Leave all your worries with him (God), because he cares for you. GNB.

Isaiah 26:3 You keep him in perfect peace whose mind is stayed on you, because he trusts in you.

John 14:1 "Let not your hearts be troubled. Believe in God; believe also in me (Jesus)."

Notes:

Worship

Worship is focussing on the greatness, the glory and the supreme work of God and responding to Him in adoration and awe.

We were made for worship – in glorifying God we complete ourselves.

There are many who work at their play, and play at their worship.

Psalm 95:6 Oh come, let us worship and bow down; let us kneel before the LORD, our Maker!

Psalm 22:27 All nations will remember the LORD. From every part of the world they will turn to him; all races will worship him. GNB.

Notes:

December 23rd

Worship

There can be no true worship of God where there is no readiness for inward change.

Worship is the specific act of ascribing to God the glory, majesty, honour and worthiness which are His. *J. Bridges*

Worship is inner health made audible.

Worship's leading characteristic is obedience.

John 4:23,24 But the hour is coming, and is now here, when the true worshippers will worship the Father in spirit and truth, for the Father is seeking such people to worship him. God is spirit, and those who worship him must worship in spirit and truth.

Notes:

Worship

There is no true knowledge of God without the worship of God.

In the process of worship, God communicates His presence to men.

C. S. Lewis

If we don't see God correctly, then we will not be able to worship Him correctly.

Rev. 14:7 He (an angel) said in a loud voice, "Honour God and praise his greatness! For the time has come for him to judge. Worship him who made heaven, earth, sea, and the springs of water!" GNB.

Psalm 96:9 Worship the LORD in the splendour of holiness;

Notes:

December 25th

Worship

Worship is the submission of all our nature to God. It is the quickening of conscience by His holiness, the nourishment of mind with His truth, the purifying of the imagination by His beauty, the opening of the heart by His love.

Archbishop William Temple

(Continued tomorrow)

Rev. 22:9 ". . . I (an angel) am a servant together with you (John) and with your brothers the prophets and with all those who obey the words in this book. Worship God!" GNB.

Deut. 11:16 Take care lest your heart be deceived, and you turn aside and serve other gods and worship them;

Notes:

Worship

(Continued from yesterday)

It is the surrender of the will to His purpose, and all this is gathered up in adoration to the most selfless emotion of which our nature is capable, and therefore the chief remedy for that self-centredness which is the original sin and the source of all actual sin.

Archbishop William Temple

Psalm 29:2 Ascribe to the LORD the glory due his name; worship the LORD in the splendour of holiness.

Romans 12:1 So then, my (Paul) brothers and sisters, because of God's great mercy to us I appeal to you: offer yourselves as a living sacrifice to God, dedicated to his service and pleasing to him. This is the true worship that you should offer. GNB.

Notes:

December 27th

Worship

Worship is an attitude of the heart, not a position of the body.

Worship is ascribing proper worth to God, exalting Him and regarding Him as being deserving of adoration and honour.

Worship is the response of a heart in love with God.

Matthew 4:10 Then Jesus said to him, "Be gone, Satan! For it is written, You shall worship the Lord your God and him only shall you serve."

Phil. 3:3 For we (brothers) are the real circumcision, who worship by the Spirit of God and glory in Christ Jesus and put no confidence in the flesh -

---

Notes:

Worship

The purpose of worship is to please God.

Worship is easier to describe than define.

Worship is giving God his rightful due. It is enjoying God.

Daniel 3:28 The King (Nebuchadnezzar) said, "Praise the God of Shadrach, Meshach, and Abednego! He sent his angel and rescued these men who serve and trust him. They disobeyed my orders and risked their lives rather than bow down and worship any god except their own." GNB.

Notes:

December 29th

Worship

Worship is leaving the pressure of life in God's hands and taking time to look at His face.

One of the most important keys to effective worship is a clear conscience.

All service is worship, and all worship is service.

Hebrews 12:28,29 Let us be thankful, then, because we receive a kingdom that cannot be shaken. Let us be grateful and worship God in a way that will please him, with reverence and awe; because our God is indeed a destroying fire. GNB.

Notes:

Worship

Worship is our adoring response to all that God is, all that God does, and all that God says. Worship means being so caught up in the glory and greatness of God that everything else seems insignificant. When our worship of God is what it ought to be, then the rest of life falls into place.

---

1 Chron. 16:29 Ascribe to the LORD the glory due his name; bring an offering and come before him! Worship the LORD in the splendour of holiness;

Psalm 100:4 Enter his gates with thanksgiving, and his courts with praise! Give thanks to him; bless his name!

Notes:

December 31st

Wrath

Wrath is the product of God's justice.

Wrath is the Holiness of God stirred into activity against sin.

Wrath is the eternal detestation of all unrighteousness – the displeasure and indignation of divine equity against evil.

A. W. Pink

Wrath is always judicial.

The thunderbolts of God's wrath are quenched in Christ's blood.

Proverbs 15:1 A soft answer turns away wrath, but a harsh word stirs up anger.

Romans 1:18 For the wrath of God is revealed from heaven against all ungodliness and unrighteousness of men, who by their unrighteousness suppress the truth.

Notes:

Personal Prayer Diary

January & February

March & April

May & June

July & August

September & October

November & December

Index